Nicotine

Other Books in the History of Drugs series:

Nicotine

Emma Carlson-Berne, Book Editor

GREENHAVEN PRESS
An imprint of Thomson Gale, a part of The Thomson Corporation

Detroit • New York • San Francisco • San Diego • New Haven, Conn.
Waterville, Maine • London • Munich

Bonnie Szumski, *Publisher*
Helen Cothran, *Managing Editor*

© 2006 Thomson Gale, a part of The Thomson Corporation.

Thomson and Star Logo are trademarks and Gale and Greenhaven Press are registered trademarks used herein under license.

For more information, contact:
Greenhaven Press
27500 Drake Rd.
Farmington Hills, MI 48331-3535
Or you can visit our Internet site at http://www.gale.com

LIBRARY OF CONGRESS CATALOGING-IN-PUBLICATION DATA

Nicotine / Emma Carlson-Berne, book editor.
    p. cm. -- (The history of drugs)
    Includes bibliographical references and index. 0-7377-2847-7 (alk. paper)
    1. Tobacco use--History. 2. Tobacco use--United States--History. 3. Nicotine--
History. 4. Nicotine addiction--History. 5. Tobacco industry--United States--
History. I. Carlson-Berne, Emma. II. Series.
    HG5730.N53 2006
    362.29'60973--dc22
                                                                    2005052803

Printed in the United States of America
10 9 8 7 6 5 4 3 2 1

Contents

In 1912, as smoking became more widespread, a forward-thinking doctor warned of the dangers of nicotine.

Chapter Three: Government Efforts to Prevent Nicotine Addiction, 1960–2000

gress for strict legislation limiting the advertising of cigarettes.

Chapter Four: Current Issues and Controversies

Foreword

Drugs are chemical compounds that affect the functioning of the body and the mind. While the U.S. Food, Drug, and Cosmetic Act defines drugs as substances intended for use in the cure, mitigation, treatment, or prevention of disease, humans have long used drugs for recreational and religious purposes as well as for healing and medicinal purposes. Depending on context, then, the term drug provokes various reactions. In recent years, the widespread problem of substance abuse and addiction has often given the word drug a negative connotation. Nevertheless, drugs have made possible a revolution in the way modern doctors treat disease. The tension arising from the myriad ways drugs can be used is what makes their history so fascinating. Positioned at the intersection of science, anthropology, religion, therapy, sociology, and cultural studies, the history of drugs offers intriguing insights on medical discovery, cultural conflict, and the bright and dark sides of human innovation and experimentation.

Drugs are commonly grouped in three broad categories: over-the-counter drugs, prescription drugs, and illegal drugs. A historical examination of drugs, however, invites students and interested readers to observe the development of these categories and to see how arbitrary and changeable they can be. A particular drug's status is often the result of social and political forces that may not necessarily reflect its medicinal effects or its potential dangers. Marijuana, for example, is currently classified as an illegal Schedule I substance by the U.S. federal government, defining it as a drug with a high potential for abuse and no currently accepted medical use. Yet in 1850 it was included in the U.S. Pharmacopoeia as a medicine, and solutions and tinctures containing cannabis were frequently prescribed for relieving pain and inducing sleep. In the 1930s, after smokable marijuana had gained notoriety as a recreational intoxicant, the Federal Bureau of Narcotics launched a misinformation campaign against the drug, claiming that it commonly induced insanity and murderous violence. While today's medical experts no longer make such claims about marijuana, they continue to disagree about the drug's long-term effects and medicinal potential. Most interestingly, several states have passed medical marijuana initiatives, which allow seriously ill patients compassionate access to the drug under state law—although these patients can still be prosecuted for marijuana use under federal law. Marijuana's illegal status, then, is not as fixed or final as the federal government's current schedule might suggest. Examining marijuana from a historical perspective offers readers the chance to develop a more sophisticated and critically informed view of a controversial and politically charged subject. It also encourages students to learn about aspects of medicine, history, and culture that may receive scant attention in textbooks.

Each book in Greenhaven's The History of Drugs series chronicles a particular substance or group of related drugs—discussing the appearance and earliest use of the drug in initial chapters and more recent and contemporary controversies in later chapters. With the incorporation of both primary and secondary sources written by physicians, anthropologists, psychologists, historians, social analysts, and lawmakers, each anthology provides an engaging panoramic view of its subject. Selections include a variety of readings, including book excerpts, government documents, newspaper editorials, academic articles, and personal narratives. The editors of each volume aim to include accounts of notable incidents, ideas, subcultures, or individuals connected with the drug's history as well as perspectives on the effects, benefits, dangers, and legal status of the drug.

Every volume in the series includes an introductory essay that presents a broad overview of the drug in question. The annotated table of contents and comprehensive index help readers quickly locate material of interest. Each selection is prefaced by a summary of the article that also provides any necessary historical context and biographical information on the author. Several other research aids are also present, including excerpts of supplementary material, a time line of relevant historical events, the U.S. government's current drug schedule, a fact sheet detailing drug effects, and a bibliography of helpful sources.

Greenhaven Press's The History of Drugs series gives readers a unique and informative introduction to an often-ignored facet of scientific and cultural history. The contents of each anthology provide a valuable resource for general readers as well as for students interested in medicine, political science, philosophy, and social studies.

Introduction

Nicotine is the primary psychoactive ingredient in the leaves of the tobacco plant *Nicotiana tabacum*. These leaves are picked and dried, or "cured." To ingest the nicotine, a user can then either chew the leaves to extract the juices, inhale powdered leaves up the nose a pinch at a time (this mostly obsolete method is commonly referred to as "taking snuff"), or light the leaves in various receptacles such as pipes or rolled paper (cigarettes) and inhale the smoke into the mouth and lungs. This last method is the most common. A person can also ingest nicotine by chewing gum containing nicotine, by wearing a transdermal nicotine patch that allows the drug to be absorbed by the skin, or by inhaling nicotine through a vapor inhaler.

Nicotine is both physically and psychologically addictive. The user's brain physically craves the drug in order to stimulate its pleasure centers, and the user psychologically craves the routines and sensations associated with the act of smoking. Thomas Schelling, the former director of the Institute for the Study of Smoking Behavior and Policy describes nicotine as one of the most addictive substances available. The nicotine in cigarette smoke provides a physical sensation in less than ten seconds after inhaling and a high that only lasts while a person is smoking, Schelling notes. Nicotine has the distinct quality of acting as both a depressant and a stimulant—a smoker may use a cigarette to help wake up in the morning and to relax before going to sleep at night. Tobacco use is by far the most common way in which a user can ingest nicotine.

The Dangers of Nicotine

Smoking tobacco has long been one of the world's most well-loved and—for good reason—thoroughly maligned habits. More than forty years after the U.S. surgeon general's first report publicizing the dangers of smoking in 1964, the ingestion of nicotine has been found to cause cancer in almost every area in the body. Smoking has been shown to cause heart disease, stroke, asthma, birth defects, and early death. In addition, chewing tobacco causes gruesome cancers in the mouth, lips, and throat that can spread to the rest of the body. According to some experts, smoking for one year shaves ten years off of a person's life expectancy. Smoking by pregnant women increases the risk of stillborn babies.

Six hundred years after the first Europeans lit bundles of dried, shredded tobacco and inhaled the smoke, society is finally beginning to understand the risks of nicotine addiction and smoking. Smoking indoors is banned in entire countries, including Ireland, Scotland, and Iceland. Forty-six states in the United States have sued the tobacco industry for the health care costs of tobacco users and won approximately $206 billion. Antismoking groups targeting children, teenagers, women, men, African Americans, Latinos, Asian Americans, and veterans work to keep these groups from smoking and to help them quit. Media stories addressing the growing research on the dangers of smoking have become frequent, contributing to society's increasingly negative view of the habit.

For many who have grown up in a post–World War II era, these antismoking measures make a great deal of sense and require little explanation. Yet for centuries negative opinions about smoking and tobacco were far from the norm. On the contrary, throughout history various groups of people have esteemed tobacco as a wonderful substance, the essence of religious worship, a valuable currency, and a symbol of freedom, independence, and friendship recognized around the world.

The Beginnings of Nicotine

The story of nicotine begins on the continent of North America, long before the European explorers arrived. For centuries Native Americans grew, cured, and smoked tobacco with a reverence as yet unmatched in history. The soothing qualities of the smoke and the renewed energy that smoking provided had deep spiritual implications for the various tribes. Tobacco was part of every life-cycle ritual and was treated as a sacred gift from the deities.

The European explorers who came to the New World in the fifteenth century with Christopher Columbus and other leaders saw the tobacco plant in a completely different, yet no less favorable, light. Sailors obtained the shredded, dried tobacco in trade from the Native Americans and took it back to Europe. Tobacco was cultivated and the smoking habit quickly began to spread. Nobles adopted the practice from the returning explorers and even Queen Elizabeth I became fond of a pipe or two after supper. Few spoke out against the habit. One exception was British satirist Samuel Rowlands, who wrote, "But this same poison, steeped India weed/ In head, heart, lungs, do the soot and cobwebs breed/ With that he gasped, and breathed out such a smoke/ That all the standers-by were like to choke."[1] However, statements like these had virtually no impact on the general public's new obsession.

The Cultivation of Tobacco

As the popularity of tobacco spread in Europe, the first colonies in Virginia and Maryland began to cultivate the plant on a greater scale, and tobacco became an extremely valuable currency. The plant was the single most important cash crop grown in the colonies for export to Europe, and the economy of the colonies revolved around its cultivation and regulation. Colonists could pay their taxes in tobacco, offer wedding dowries of tobacco, and obtain goods and services using tobacco in lieu of money.

When the colonies won their independence and plantations expanded, tobacco farming became increasingly dependent on slave labor but remained the main cash crop in the southern United States. Tobacco took its place beside cotton as one of the crops indelibly associated with the practice of slavery. When the Civil War ended, some tobacco plantations were able to survive by implementing sharecropping systems. Many other farmers, however, found themselves farming much smaller plots of land for much less profit.

Smoking as a Universal Habit

Tobacco's popularity remained strong throughout the latter half of the nineteenth century. Pipes were practically ubiquitous among men, though smoking for women was considered uncouth, particularly among the upper classes. Still, there were few, if any, murmurs about the health risks of tobacco. In fact, tobacco was believed to confer significant health *benefits*. Tobacco was seen as an excellent purifier for lungs and minds. The nineteenth-century edition of the *Merck Medical Manual* recommended smoking for cases of asthma and bronchitis. By the end of the 1800s most health claims had been disproved; however, tobacco's popularity did not diminish.

The twentieth century became the century of the cigarette. By now America had used tobacco for three hundred years. As the pace of life continued to hasten during the early years of the 1900s, the portability and convenience of the cigarette increased its popularity. In the wake of the women's suffrage movement, smoking by women became more socially acceptable. In addition, cigarettes were included in soldiers' rations during World War I, virtually guaranteeing that an entire generation came home from war addicted to nicotine. The U.S. Department of Agriculture declared tobacco an essential crop during World War II to ensure plenty of cigarettes for the troops abroad. It was common practice for soldiers in the field to hold a cigarette to the lips of a dying comrade to offer some last pleasure. During the liberation of the concentration camps in Europe, the starving prisoners were offered water and chocolate—and cigarettes, which had become the universal symbol for friendship and trade. An American veteran describes the value of cigarettes on the black market in Europe during World War II:

Just to put things in perspective, cigarettes were the most desirable commodity in Europe at the time. They had become a medium of exchange and in many cases, people would rather be paid in American cigarettes than in money from any country. They could be bartered for anything and were more in demand than currencies. No matter what you paid for them, if you tried hard enough, you could always make a profit on them. If you sold a pack, the next question always was, "Do you have any more?"[2]

Smoking's Decline

Although cigarettes came to be viewed as an essential commodity in the first half of the twentieth century, in the second half the popularity of tobacco began to diminish in the United States. Medical research showing the connection between smoking and disease was highly publicized. Further, people were outraged when it became clear that the tobacco industry had deliberately engaged in deceptive advertising, had added extra nicotine to cigarettes despite knowledge of its dangers, and had targeted youth in marketing for decades to ensure future generations of nicotine addicts.

Soon after World War II smoking began the decline from which it has yet to recover. In 1950 medical researcher and physician Morton Levin published the first major medical study linking smoking to lung cancer in the *Journal of the American Medical Association*. Several other studies revealing further dangers of smoking soon followed. In 1952 writer Ray Norr published an article entitled "Cancer by the Carton" in the *Reader's Digest* magazine, which at the time had a worldwide circulation of 30.5 million. In 1964 the U.S. surgeon general Luther Terry issued a landmark report, "Smoking and Health," providing the first government recognition that cigarette smoking causes cancer and other serious diseases. For the first time, people began to understand the link between smoking and cancer.

Many of the tobacco control efforts during the next three decades can be attributed to the influence of the 1964 report. Increasingly, federal and state governments began to actively regulate tobacco use. In 1971 the Richard M. Nixon administration signed a federal order banning tobacco advertising on broadcast media. Beginning in 1983 state governments began to enact unprecedented laws to create smoke-free public places, restaurants, and bars. Still, smoking remained widely socially acceptable.

Current Issues

Beginning in the early 1990s, a series of revelations about the practices of tobacco companies reenergized the backlash against nicotine. In 1991 the *Journal of the American Medical Association* found that approximately 90 percent of preschool students could identify "Joe Camel," a cartoon character who appeared in ads for Camel cigarettes. Though the company which manufactures Camels, R.J. Reynolds, was cleared of targeting youth by the Federal Trade Commission (FTC) in 1994, the industry as a whole was damaged by the report. Compounding the negative media attention, in 1994 papers were delivered anonymously to San Francisco researcher Stanton Glantz that showed that tobacco company Brown & Williamson had concealed its findings about the addictive qualities of nicotine and lied to society for decades. The "B&W" papers were published in the *Journal of the American Medical Association* in July 1995 and eventually published on the Internet. In addition, the FTC renewed its focus on Joe Camel in 1997, lodging a formal accusation against the advertising practices of manufacturer R.J. Reynolds.

The last decade of the twentieth century was also an active period of litigation and government regulation that aimed to dismantle much of the power structure the tobacco industry had built. In 1994 the tobacco industry experienced one of the most significant upheavals in its history when forty-six states joined in a four-year period of litigation against the industry, suing to recover decades of health care costs lost due to smoking. Since then class action lawsuits have been brought against the industry by various groups: smokers themselves, the states mentioned above, and health plans such as Blue Cross. In 1999 the federal government sued the industry to recoup health care costs under racketeering laws.[3] In June 2004 the federal government also began to implement regulations to end seventy years of price supports for tobacco farmers over a ten-year period.

All of the negative publicity about smoking has led to a rapid decline in the number of smokers—whereas 50 percent of adult Americans smoked during the 1970s, by the first decade of the twenty-first century, only about 25 percent of adult Americans are smokers. Despite the decrease in the number of smokers, each year approximately 440,000 people die from diseases linked to smoking. Public health advocates therefore continue to work to prevent people from becoming addicted to nicotine and to pass laws aimed at discouraging smoking. Twenty-three states have one or more cities with comprehensive smoking bans that include most indoor facilities. For most of society, tobacco's long history has reached a low point. Once a sacred and precious commodity, tobacco today is viewed by most people, including smokers, as an addictive and dangerous substance.

Notes

1. Samuel Rowlands, "A Woeful Exclamation Late I Heard," in *The Letting of Humours Blood in the Head Veine,* 1600. Spelling has been updated by the editor.
2. Robert F. Gallagher, "Black Market," in *World War II Story by Robert F. Gallagher.* www.gallagher.com.
3. At the time of writing, a decision in the case was pending.

CHAPTER 1

Early Uses and Views

Nicotine and Early Native Americans

Jason Hughes

Jason Hughes is a lecturer at the Center for Labor Market Studies at the University of Leicester in England. In this excerpt from his book Learning to Smoke: Tobacco Use in the West, *he provides an overview of the role of tobacco in the lives of Native Americans prior to and during their encounters with the early European explorers. As Hughes writes, for these tribes, using tobacco was much more than simply a way to relax or relieve stress. The growing, cultivating, and smoking of tobacco was integral to spiritual and cultural beliefs and central to religious worship, in which spirits had to be appeased with regular offerings of tobacco smoke. In ways the Europeans never fully understood, the power of tobacco in Native American society was difficult to overstate, Hughes observes.*

As a psychoactive plant, tobacco lay at the heart of many [early] Native American belief systems. Indigenous societies made use of seven to eight times more narcotic plants than the Old World, and a large number of these had been in more or less continual use since the earliest habitation of the Americas. Characteristic of Native American understandings of social reality was the belief that hallucinogenic plants joined the natural and supernatural worlds. These plants were sacred; they were understood to house spiritual beings and to facilitate altered states of consciousness essential to communication with the spirit world.

Along with the supernatural powers ascribed to tobacco, the plant was understood to have supernatural origins. In fact, a remarkable recurrence of theme is found in various Native

Jason Hughes, *Learning to Smoke: Tobacco Use in the West.* Chicago: University of Chicago Press, 2003. Copyright © 2003 by the University of Chicago Press. Reproduced by permission of the publisher and author.

American origin myths concerning the tobacco plant. Typical in such myths is the notion that tobacco was given to humans as a resource that could be exchanged with the spirits. Spirits were understood to have an endless longing for tobacco, which went beyond a mere attraction to its aroma and taste: more fundamentally, these beings were seen to need tobacco for their sustenance and survival. Since they could not grow tobacco for themselves, spirits were understood to be dependent on humans to supply them. Thus it was understood that humans and spirits were locked into a fundamental interdependence that hinged on the use of tobacco.

The Hunger of the Spirits

The "hunger" for tobacco experienced by Native American tobacco users was perceived as the hunger and longing of the spirits. Tobacco was used to appease the spiritual hunger, thereby gaining favors and good fortune. This was achieved not only through the direct consumption of tobacco, such as smoking or chewing, but also through ritual tobacco offerings and invocations. The following account taken from an ethnography of seventeenth-century Huron peoples typifies traditional Native American understandings of the spiritual role of tobacco:

> The Huron believed that animate spirits resided in the earth, the rivers, lakes, certain rocks, and the sky and had control over journeying, trading, war, feasts, disease, and other matters. To appease and obtain the favor of these spirits, tobacco was thrown into the fire and a prayer said. If, for example, the offering was to implore health, they would say, *taenguiaens,* "Heal me." ... Tobacco frequently was used in ritual contexts and offered to the spirits with a prayer. In addition to those occasions ..., it was thrown into the water of a great lake in order to calm it and to appease a spirit *(Iannoa)* who, in despair, once cast himself into a lake and who caused ... storms. Before going to sleep a man might throw some tobacco on the fire and pray to the spirits to

take care of his house. It was offered to some rocks that the Huron passed when going to Quebec to trade. One of these was called *hihihouray*, 'a rock where the owl makes its nest' . . . they stopped and put tobacco into one of the clefts saying, *aki ca ichikhon condayee aenwaen ondayee d'aonstaancwas, etc.*, "spirit who dwellest in this place, here is some tobacco which I present you; help us, guard us from shipwreck, defend us from our enemies, and cause that after having made good trades we may return safe and sound to our villages."[Elizabeth Tooker, 1964]

Power and Prestige

Tobacco had such symbolic value and significance that, among some Native American peoples, those who merely planted and nurtured tobacco attained high prestige and honor. The Crow Nation are a particularly good example in this respect. Despite the fact that the Crow were "roving peoples," since their very earliest times they had cultivated tobacco. They had carefully maintained a consistent strain by preserving the seed from one crop to the next, in keeping with what they believed were their ancestors' wishes. [According to anthropologist Edward Denig] it was understood by the Crow that without the seed, leaf, and blossom of their particular tobacco, their nation would "pass away from the face of the earth." Those who continued this tobacco-planting tradition were said to be endowed with a wide range of supernatural powers: "bring rain, avert pestilence, control the wind, conquer disease, make the buffalo come near their camp, and increase the number of all kinds of game; . . . in fact bring about any event not dependent upon ordinary human possibility." The few people who were involved with the tradition were keen to hold on to their superior power, status, and standing and the considerable resources the position afforded. Indeed, there was an extensive ordeal involved with attaining the right to join their elite ranks:

> Sometimes, with a view to acquiring property, one of them will sell his right or powers to some aspiring individual. In

this case the candidate gives everything he has in the world—all his horses, dresses, arms, even his lodge and household utensils—to pay for the great medicine and honor to become a Tobacco Planter. On an occasion of this kind the applicant is adopted with great ceremonies into the band of Planters. His flesh is cut and burned in large and deep furrows around the breast and along his arms, leaving for a long time dangerous and disgusting wounds difficult to heal. He is also obliged to go several days without food or water. After passing through this ordeal, he is furnished with some tobacco seed in exchange for everything he possesses. In this way the rite is perpetuated, and never has received the least check or interruption. On the contrary, it appears to become more honorable from being more ancient and from the difficulties attendant on becoming a conductor of the ceremony. [Elizabeth Denig, 1953]

European Encounters

When explorers from the Old World initially encountered tobacco among Native American peoples, they understood very little of the complex systems of beliefs that mediated and governed its use. To the earliest European travelers, and those who settled in subsequent centuries, the sight of Amerindians offering tobacco to the spirits was confusing, perhaps even comical. As [historian M.] Higler recounts:

An old Mille Lac [Native American tribe related to the Ojibwa] informant noted: "Some white men drowned here in the lake, and that did not happen for nothing. Some things are sacred to Indians and white people who make fun of it can expect to be punished. Whites have laughed at Indians putting tobacco in the lake. We put tobacco into the lake whenever we go swimming, or when we want to cross the lake. One time, long ago, we were crossing the lake in a steamboat called 'Queen Anne.' Many Indians were on the boat. We were coming from Waukon and going to the Point. The waves were so high that we thought we were going to drown. My great-grandfather threw three or four sacks of tobacco into the water and soon the waves took us back to Waukon. We were all saved."

Thus tobacco was of great significance to Native American peoples, playing a fundamental role in religious and medical practice. Their understandings of the plant led to ways of using it that were remarkably different from those characterizing present-day Western cigarette smokers and also early European users. Indeed, Europeans encountering Native American peoples had little understanding of the plant's sacred status in their cosmology.

Forms of Tobacco Use

A wide range of tobacco-consumption practices had been developed by Native American peoples long before the first Europeans made contact. Tobacco was snuffed as a dry powder; chewed; drunk by ingesting the juice of the tobacco plant; licked by rubbing a syrupy tobacco extract along the gums and teeth; absorbed locally as an analgesic by applying the leaves or leaf extracts to cuts, bites, stings, and other wounds; absorbed ocularly by applying tobacco leaf or leaf extracts to the surface of the eye; and injected anally as an enema. However, by far the most popular mode of tobacco consumption was smoking. There are several reasons for this. First, tobacco [smoking] was the most effective means of nicotine absorption. If we accept—for the moment, at least—the primacy of nicotine as a pharmacological agent in tobacco and as a factor in generating the experience of tobacco use, it follows that smoking would prevail as a mode of tobacco consumption. Second, tobacco smoke had a high degree of symbolic potency: the rising smoke was believed to symbolize an ascending petition to the spirits. Symbolic associations with fire and heat may have also been significant. The indigenous peoples of North America generally smoked through pipes, while those of South America favored cigars and an early form of cigarettes, dried tobacco leaves in a corn-husk wrapper.

King James's Antismoking Crusade

King James I

King James I ruled Britain from 1567 to 1625 and was responsible for the best-known translation of the Old and New Testaments, the King James Bible. In 1604 James also became the world's first antismoking activist when he condemned the new habit sweeping his kingdom in a pamphlet entitled A Counterblaste to Tobacco, *which is extracted in this selection. Tobacco had recently made the journey with European explorers across the ocean from the New World, where it had been discovered in use by Native Americans. Smoking had become popular among all classes of Englishmen (at the time, women did not participate in the pastime of smoking). King James, however, regarded smoking, which he called "taking tobacco," as disgusting—primarily, it seems, because it was linked with Native Americans and their use of tobacco as a cure for smallpox. Desperately, he pleads with his subjects to stop smoking and thus curtail their association with the habits of the "savages." This selection has been transcribed into modern English by the editor.*

And surely in my opinion, there cannot be a more base and yet, hurtful corruption in a country, than is this vile use (or other abuse) of taking tobacco in this kingdom, which has moved me, shortly to discover the abuses thereof in this following little pamphlet.

If any think it a light argument, so is it but a toy that is bestowed upon you. And since the subject is but of smoke, I think the fume of an idle brain, may serve for a sufficient battery against so fumious [hotheaded] and feeble an enemy. If my grounds be found true, it is all I look for; but if they carry

King James I, "A Counterblaste to Tobacco," transcribed by R.S. Bear from *James I Essayes in Poesie, 1585 and A Counterblaste to Tobacco, 1604,* reprint edited by Edward Arber, 1869.

the force of persuasion with them, it is all I can wish, and more than I can expect. My only care is that you, my dear country-men, may rightly conceive even by this smallest trifle, of the sincerity of my meaning in greater matters, never to spare any pain, that my tend to the procuring of your weal [happiness] and prosperity.

Tobacco Use by Native Americans

That the manifold abuses of this vile custom of tobacco taking, may the better by espied, it is fit, that first you enter into consideration both of the first original thereof, and likewise of the reasons of the first entry into this country. For certainly as such customs, that have their first institution either from a godly, necessary, or honorable ground, and are first brought in, by the means of some worthy, virtuous, and great personage, are ever, and most justly, held in great and reverent estimation and account, by all wise, virtuous, and temperate spirits: So should it by the contrary, justly bring a great disgrace into that sort of customs, which having their original from base corruption and barbarity, do in like sort, make their first entry into a country, by an inconsiderate and childish affectation of novelty, as is the true case of the first invention of tobacco taking, and of the first entry thereof among us. For tobacco being a common herb, which (though under diverse names) grows almost everywhere, was first found out by some of the barbarous Indians, to be a preservative, or antidote against the pocks [smallpox], a filthy disease, whereunto these barbarous people are (as all men know) very much subject, what through the uncleanly and adust constitution of their bodies, and what through the intemperate heat of their climate: so that as from them was first brought into Christendom, that most detestable disease, so from them likewise was brought this use of tobacco, as a stinking and unsavory Antidote, for so corrupted and execrable a malady, the stinking suffumigation [to apply fumes to the body] whereof the yet use against that disease, making so one canker [source of decay] of venom to eat out another.

And now good country-men let us (I pray you) consider, what honor or policy can move us to imitate the barbarous and beastly manners of the wild, godless, and slavish Indians, especially in so vile and stinking a custom? Shall we that disdain to imitate the manners of our neighbor France (having the style of the first Christian kingdom) and that cannot endure the spirit of the Spaniards (their king being now comparable in the largeness of dominions to the great emperor of Turkey)? Shall we, I say, that have been so long civil and wealthy in peace, famous and invincible in war, fortunate in both, we that have been ever able to aide any of our neighbors (but never deafed any of their ears with any of our supplications for assistance) shall we, I say, without blushing, abase our selves so far, as to imitate these beastly Indians, slaves to the Spaniards, refuse to the world, and as yet aliens from the holy covenant of God? Why do we not as well imitate them in walking naked as they do? In preferring glasses, feathers, and such toys, to gold and precious stones, as they do? Yea, why do we not deny God and adore the devil, as they do?

Tobacco Use Continues

Now the corrupted baseness of the first use of this tobacco, does very well agree the foolish and groundless first entry thereof into this kingdom. It is not so long since the first entry of this abuse amongst us here, as this present age cannot yet very well remember, both the first author, and the form of the first introduction of it amongst us. It was neither brought in by king, great conqueror, nor learned doctor of physic [medicine].

With the report of a great discovery for a conquest, some two or three savage men, were brought in, together with the savage custom. But the pity is, the poor wild barbarous men died, but that vile barbarous custom is yet alive, yea in fresh

KING JAMES I

vigor, so as it seems a miracle to me, how a custom springing from so vile a ground, and brought in by a father so generally hated, should be welcomed upon so slender a warrant. For if they that first put it in practice here, had remembered for what respect it was used by them from whence it came, I am sure they would have been loath, to have taken so far the imputation of that disease upon them as they did, by using the cure thereof. . . . Counter-poisons are never used but where poison is thought to precede.

But since it is true, that diverse customs slightly grounded and with no better warrant entered in a commonwealth, may yet in the use of them thereafter, prove both necessary and profitable; it is therefore next to be examined, if there be not a full sympathy and true proportion, between the base ground and foolish entry, and the loathsome, and hurtful use of this stinking antidote.

I am now therefore heartily to pray you consider, first upon what false and erroneous grounds you have first built the general good liking thereof, and next what sins towards God, and foolish vanities before the world you commit, in the detestable use of it.

Tobacco During America's Colonial Period

Gary M. Pecquet

Gary M. Pecquet is a visiting assistant professor of economics at Tulane University in Louisiana. In the following article Pecquet analyzes the economic effects of regulation on tobacco farming in colonial Virginia. By the 1600s, he notes, tobacco was the major cash crop in the colonies, taking the place of gold as currency. However, occasionally Virginia would experience a "tobacco bust" when farmers raised especially abundant crops and the price of tobacco fell. As Pecquet explains, Virginia's colonial assembly began to restrict the number of tobacco plants farmers could grow in order to prevent the price of tobacco from falling. This crop control scheme did not benefit the farmers in the long run because they ended up spending more money trying to increase the productivity of each tobacco plant. Moreover, the colonists increased tensions with local Indian tribes when they cleared additional lands next to streams—areas that produced the highest quality tobacco.

The British colonized Virginia in 1607, and by 1612 they were growing tobacco. It soon became the colony's major export. But heavy reliance upon tobacco proved troublesome for the Virginians. Small changes in the supply could produce large changes in tobacco's price.

The tugs of demand and supply altered the price of tobacco and produced the "trade cycle" of the Chesapeake Bay colonies. Under British mercantilist [commercial] law, all tobacco had to be shipped directly to England. English merchants marketed the tobacco products to the rest of the world. As new markets were opened and new uses for tobacco were discovered, the demand for tobacco increased and so did the price. A "tobacco boom" in Virginia would be followed by increased migration to the colony. This in turn led to an increase in supply, depressing the price and ending the boom.

Occasionally a "tobacco bust" occurred when favorable weather fostered overproduction and slashed tobacco prices. Sometimes war severed the colonies from their markets, which also hurt the growers. During the 17th century the overall trend for tobacco prices was down, as the colonists learned better cultivating techniques.

From time to time, colonial authorities imposed crop restrictions upon the growers. The chief purpose of these regulations was to maintain an "adequate" price for tobacco in much the same way that crop controls and price supports do in 20th-century America. In both cases crop restrictions may enrich the farmers, but only at the expense of consumers. Moreover, since restrictions discourage or destroy production, a net decrease in wealth results.

What farmers needed then ... was insurance to protect them against uncertainty in the prices of their products. Today, this might be achieved through the commodity futures markets. In the 17th century, Virginians could purchase bills of exchange. These bills entitled the holder to buy merchandise on credit. The prices of tobacco and bills of exchange varied inversely, since the bills amounted to claims upon future merchandise that colonists could purchase with the present tobacco crop. By altering his portfolio, a colonist could effectively insure his assets.

Restrictions on Tobacco Plants

The colonial assembly began to restrict directly the number of tobacco plants with the inspection law of 1629–1630. This law limited the number of plants to 2,000 per family member. Subsequently, these crop restrictions became more limiting. Family members not engaged in tobacco cultivation were no longer counted. Later, only nine leaves per plant could be cultivated. In 1633, the assembly reduced the maximum number of plants to 1,500 for each family member engaged in tobacco production.

These limitations drastically altered the planting habits of the Virginia colonists. The fertility of the plantations already under cultivation tended to decline with each successive planting season. This tended to reduce the size of the tobacco plants. The planters tried to improve their crops by fertilizing the lands with cattle manure. This, however, tainted the flavor of the tobacco.

The best way to comply with the crop restrictions and still maximize the value of the tobacco crop was to grow the tallest and highest quality tobacco possible. This could be done only on virgin land. By the end of 1637, the colonists discovered that the best tobacco-growing lands were along streams.

Virginia planters hastily attempted to secure the new land before gaining legal title. They intended to retain their old land and homes while cultivating the new ground with their legal quotas of tobacco plants. The primary costs of securing the land included the expenses of clearing the forests, the construction of usually unsubstantial living quarters for the workmen—and the increased danger of Indian attacks. Frontier tobacco plantations could not be easily defended by the colonial militia. Over one-third of the laborers had to be stationed on guard duty.

Almost no one would have predicted that the crop limitations of the 1630s would increase tensions with the nearby Indian tribes. Economic theory, however, predicts that whenever the government creates an artificial benefit for some group in society, people will expend resources to avail themselves of these benefits. Thus, if the government attempts to support agricultural producers by imposing a price floor on farm products, farmers tend to grow more crops. If the government doesn't wish to stockpile farm produce, it must then restrict agricultural production. It can limit acreage, but this encourages farmers to work the allowable acres more intensively. It can limit the number of plants in the field, as did the Virginia colonial assembly, but this only induces the farmers to increase their production costs in other ways which maximize the value of each plant instead of cultivating many smaller plants. These costs may be incurred due to increased fertilization, relocation, and so on.

Regulations Lead to Disaster

Basic economics argues that, in the long run, additional costs of production will arise to eliminate the benefits of crop restrictions to the recipients. It worked this way in 17th-century Virginia. . . . Only the particular manner in which these expenses manifested themselves—in the form of increased risk of Indian attacks—was unusual. Moreover, as costly as these crop restrictions were, they did not prevent the decline in tobacco prices. By 1639, the price of tobacco dropped below subsistence levels. The colonial authorities passed new regulations that permitted destruction of a large part of the crop. This policy too, produced only disaster. It not only destroyed the fruits of over half of Virginia's productive resources, to the extent that it did support tobacco prices it encouraged more lands to be brought under cultivation.

Throughout its colonial history, Virginia attempted many other crop control schemes. After the 1630s, most of them proved ineffective for yet another reason. Maryland became a major competitor in growing tobacco. Any restriction of the Virginia crop could be replaced by increased production from its neighbor. Crop restriction schemes required collusion between the two colonies. The Maryland economy, however, was more diversified than Virginia's. The many non-tobacco growers were unlikely to vote for measures designed to increase the price of tobacco when they had to obtain the weed in order to pay their taxes and settle their debt accounts. Thus, the Maryland assembly seldom approved crop restriction proposals. Competition replaced monopoly in the field of tobacco production.

A Victorian View of Smoking

An English Doctor

In the nineteenth century, smoking was as socially acceptable and widespread as chewing gum is in the twenty-first century. However, some people were concerned about the rampant use of tobacco. In the following selection first published in 1879, a British doctor acknowledges the obsessive nature of the habit for some smokers but also argues in favor of tobacco use. Reflecting the scientific knowledge of the day, the doctor points out that smoking does not shorten the life span, cause coughs or heart trouble, or provoke hand tremors or blindness—all common concerns of the antismoking activists of the period. Rather, the writer argues, smoking is an excellent expectorant and refreshes a tired mind and body. He notes that while the young should avoid the habit, and no one should smoke before breakfast, in general smoking is a pleasant and possibly beneficial practice.

As a medical man, I am constantly coming in contact with men who are perfect victims to the abuse of tobacco, whose mind and body are alike suffering from this excess. Such men are a nuisance to society, and take no enjoyment in anything unless tobacco plays a part in the performance. These men think a dinner party a martyrdom, because it means some hours' deprivation of tobacco; a ball is not to be tolerated; a lecture or scientific meeting is an abomination; anything, in short, which may in the least degree interfere with the craved-for pipe is looked upon with aversion. These men begin to smoke immediately after breakfast, often before, and lose no opportunity during the day of indulging, irrespective of place, company, or consideration for others—frequently, indeed, sitting up late into the night to continue their practice. I have met with some strange instances of this bondage to tobacco. A city man that I know gets half an hour for his lun-

"An English Doctor's Plea for Smoking," *Harper's Weekly,* October 18, 1879.

cheon or dinner in the middle of the day; but he manages to eat a few biscuits during office hours, and spends his half hour walking up and down one of the quays smoking. This man walks to the city every morning from his home, the distance being three miles; he also walks home every evening, and he smokes incessantly during the walk each way. He dines at six o'clock, and then smokes without ceasing until bedtime. On Sunday he smokes all day, except during meals; he will never attend a place of worship, because it would curtail his smoking. He will never go into society with his wife, and, indeed, will not readily talk to her at home, as it disturbs his smoking. In all other respects this man is a good husband and father. Another acquaintance of mine, who is a highly intellectual and deeply read man, will tolerate nothing that may postpone his smoke. At dinner he is in a perpetual drive to get done, so as to begin his pipe; he wants no pudding, cheese, or dessert; taking these would involve loss of time, and put off the smoking period a few minutes longer. He likewise requires no tea or supper, protesting he is not hungry, and that he does not wish to be disturbed in his smoke. Another man that I know is in a government office, and when the usual public holidays occur, his treat is to lie in bed all day and smoke. The gentleman is married, and always smokes his last pipe in bed.

Smoking and Health

But is tobacco-smoking, in moderation, detrimental to health? The non-smoker declares the practice injurious, the smoker holds the contrary, and the former calls up the physiologist in support of his case, and no doubt he is a reliable witness. But this same witness will tell you that alcohol is also a poison, and yet the world smokes, and drinks, and lives! Facts must prevail against theories and arguments, and we can not deny the fact that millions of men smoke more or less, and yet maintain the highest standard of health, perform the most fatiguing bodily labor, and are capable of the highest intellectual efforts. The scientific physiologist can not settle this question. It will help us in this investigation if we reflect upon the general effects of smoking: first, upon nations, such as Germany, America, France, or England; secondly, if we take certain classes of men in these countries, such as soldiers; and thirdly, if we examine educated intelligent individuals. There are, I believe, no national statistics available as regards the average duration of life of smokers and non-smokers. It is true, however, that the age of man has not altered since tobacco was introduced in 1492, and, speaking generally, we do not find the average duration of life shorter in Germany or America, where smoking is almost universal, than it is in this country, where still a large number of the population do not smoke. Then, again, if smoking were the dreadful national poison some assert, we should find that women, who do not smoke, had a decided and easily recognized extension of life as compared with men. But such is not the case. The anti-smoker will here again meet you by saying, if the average duration of life be not curtailed by tobacco, you can not deny that it is slightly injurious to health, that it gives rise to a little dyspepsia in all cases, which lowers the general tone of the system, and thus interferes with the highest standards of national health. I do deny this. If it were the case, careful observers would, ere this, have demonstrated that the life of the smoker is not so good as that of the non-smoker. It would be totally impossible for a man day by day, and year by year, to continue in however slight a degree any injurious practice without ultimately paying the penalty in the shape of injured health and shortened life; and if such were the case, our assurance [insurance] offices would have recognized the fact, and we should have one more question added to their long list of queries for the proposing assurer [insurer], viz., "Do you smoke?" As far as one can form an opinion, there is no difference in the duration of adult male life in any country in Europe which can in the slightest degree be traced to smoking; and if we take our own country, where we find smoking habits increasing year by year, instead of any decline in the male longevity, I believe the very contrary to be the fact.

Smoking Is Safe in Moderation

Secondly, if we take groups of men in this or any other country, such as soldiers or sailors, and most carefully investigate their state of health, we shall be unable to discover anything that would lead us to believe that smoking is injurious. Now it is notorious that nearly all sailors and soldiers smoke, yet we do not find that they suffer more from amaurosis, or blindness, than an equal number of the civil population who do not smoke. Nor have I been able to learn that the so-called *smoker's heart* —a form of palpitation—is more common in the army or navy than among the general public. The same may be said about tremor of the hands, and other symptoms which arise from excess in tobacco; while as to any injury to the moral qualities, the German soldiers who fought and won the Franco-German war were smokers almost to a man, and nobody can question their remarkable courage and endurance.

Thirdly, take individuals, and ask sensible, thoughtful men who are smokers whether they have experienced any appreciable injury from the habit, and I believe the answer will be a negative. They will tell you that smoking conduces to the maintenance of mens sana in corpore sano [a sound mind in a sound body]. I am aware that men are liable to deceive themselves on such a matter, but I am speaking of men not given to self-deception. Medical men, for instance, smoke very generally, and I have been informed by several that they can do their work more easily, and feel better, if they smoke moderately; but if, from some accidental circumstance, this moderation should, on occasion, degenerate into excess, injurious symptoms follow. Let me quote one or two opinions on the subject. Sir Robert Christison writes, "No well-ascertained ill effects have been shown to result from the habitual practice of tobacco-smoking"; whilst Dr. Richardson says, "Perhaps it is the only luxury not injurious." And Dr. Pereira, one of the greatest writers on therapeutics, remarks: "In habitual smokers the practice, when moderately indulged in, produces that remarkably soothing and tranquillizing effect on the mind which has caused it to be so much adopted by all classes of society." The study of individual smokers must convince any reasonable mind that the practice is not destructive to body and mind, as some assert. Look, for instance at Prince Bismarck [of Germany] and Count Moltke [of Denmark]. They smoke continually, and yet they are two of the most remarkable men in Europe. I know that some of our greatest physicians and surgeons smoke, and also that at the bar some of the most distinguished men enjoy their cigars. How, then, can tobacco poison mind and body? I am, of course, asking this question with regard to moderate smoking. No one can be more ready than I am to admit that excess in tobacco is a great evil. But here I may be asked, What is excess? This is, I must say, an extremely difficult question to answer. What may be excess in one man is only moderation in another. There is the greatest difference as to the amount which men smoke. Just as some men can eat a heavy meat meal three times a day, and feel no symptom of indigestion, so there are many men who can smoke large quantities of tobacco without injury. I repeat that we can not exactly define the quantity any man may smoke without deleterious results, but speaking generally, and as the result of considerable observation, I believe that an adult may smoke a couple of ounces of tobacco a week, and feel sure that is not overstepping the boundary of moderation.

Health Benefits of Smoking

The chief danger of smoking is lest this moderation should degenerate into excess. But in this risk tobacco is not much different from other luxuries or indulgences. If this argument is to be used against tobacco, we must also apply it about every habit of man. I readily admit that I have seen many cases of serious injury to health from excessive smoking; but I must also add that I know many instances in which moderate smoking has proved most beneficial. It may, however, be asked, How can tobacco possibly be any advantage to health? The answer to this question is that its beneficial action is through the nervous system. Medical men well know the *sedative* action of alcohol after fatigue or severe mental effort. Just in the same way tobacco acts on some people, but not on all.

Sir James Paget, one of the greatest philosophers in the medical profession, in a recent paper writes:

> "Considering how largely our nature has been changed from that state" (the savage state) "by the gradual development of society, and by the various habits, dispositions, and capacities therewith associated, it is in the highest degree probable that with these changes we should have beneficial adjustments of different foods or other means of sustaining us in our work. Among these we may reckon the greater part of the comforts, and of what now seem to be the necessities, of our civilized, that is, our natural, state—such as wheaten bread, potatoes, cultivated fruits, and well-fed meat, and similarly among these we may reckon, unless there be clear reason to the contrary, such drinks as tea, coffee, alcoholic drinks, and, I even venture to think, tobacco, though probably for only much smaller groups of men."

I have known men so fatigued after a severe day's work as to be unable to eat food; but only let them smoke for a short while, and then they can eat and enjoy a hearty meal. Again, ask the sportsman who has missed his luncheon, and he will tell you how a pipe of tobacco will lessen the sense of fatigue, and enable him to continue his sport without food for a long time. The power of tobacco to compensate, to a certain extent, the want of food is well known.

Smoking Habits to Avoid

Tobacco has also some special advantages for some individuals. For some it acts as an expectorant, and enables many an asthmatic to breathe more comfortably. It is also well known to be of great use in cases of habitual constipation. But I believe it is its qualities as a soother of the overwrought, tired, and worried brain that have made tobacco-smoking so universal in this age of competition and excitement. I have no doubt that mental equilibrium has often been restored by the soothing influence of smoking; excitement and irritability have been calmed, the wear and tear of brain tissue has been diminished, and the mind been rescued from insanity. This is why men smoke; this is the health aspect of tobacco. It is not for the taste or the odor that we smoke, but because of the tranquillizing effect of tobacco on our nervous system; and hence the good of smoking after the day's work is over, mind and body being benefited by a moderate use of tobacco in the evening. "With the constant pipe diffusing its aroma around him, the German philosopher works out the profoundest of his works of thought." I think that smoking, like alcohol, is much more beneficial if not indulged in until the evening, when the work and worry of the day are over. Smoking in the morning, immediately after breakfast, is certainly injurious. The meal has not been digested, the system is still unnourished by the food, and is practically fasting; therefore the heart is very liable to be depressed seriously by the action of the nicotine. I know that smokers say the morning pipe is the nicest of all. It may be so; but all the same it is certainly the one most calculated to hurt the animal economy. As to its being the most enjoyable pipe, this is purely a matter of habit; and just as we have not our dinner appetite in the morning, because we are accustomed to have that meal later in the day, so with this morning smoke: if we postpone smoking until the evening, we shall soon lose the appetite for it in the morning. And here I would enter my strongest protest against smoking among boys, or during adolescence. I agree with Dr. Fothergill, that "tobacco, though a harmless associate for grown men, is a dangerous and seductive acquaintance for boys." All opinions agree that smoking is injurious before the frame is matured. The growing lad should be aware that by his indulgence he may interfere with his development as a robust man. One-and-twenty is quite soon enough for people to begin smoking, if they wish in after-years to derive benefit and not harm from the practice. And for mere boys, between fourteen and twenty, to indulge much in tobacco is complete folly. I watch with regret the number of youths who pass my house each morning smoking. They have just breakfasted, and are hurrying to the city. They smoke while going to town, and, as I explained above, are still fasting, as far as having received due nourishment from the morning meal is concerned. What happens? Why, this: When they arrive in town they feel depressed, and begin the day with a glass of "bitter," or one of dry sherry. Disastrous results to the health of these foolish youths follow sooner or later, and I promise them they will not be able to say in after-life with Shakespeare: "Though I look old, yet I am strong and lusty; For in my youth I never did apply Hot and rebellious liquors in my blood."

On the other hand, I do not think it well for middle-aged men, who have long been habitual smokers, to discontinue the practice. I believe I have seen evil results ensue. I am inclined to agree in the advice which an eminent Continental physician gave a friend of mine who consulted him, and said he was a great smoker, but had given it up. Dr. Franks advised him to begin again to smoke moderately, "as it was not wise to break with an old friend."

A Good Cigar

Mark Twain

The master of early twentieth-century commentary and humor, Samuel L. Clemens, known more commonly by his pseudonym Mark Twain, was rarely seen without a cigar in his mouth. An avid smoker all of his life, he died of heart disease at the age of seventy-four. In the following personal essay from his book What Is Man? and Other Essays, *he writes in typical humorous Twain fashion about his passionate love for the cigar. He loves cheap cigars the most, he tells the reader, and the rougher and smellier, the better. The essay is notable on two levels: First, it is an example of the fervor with which some smokers regard their habit; second, it is typical of much of the writing of the time in that Twain makes no mention of the dangers of smoking or the effects on his health. For many people in the first half of the twentieth century, the addictive quality of nicotine and tobacco simply was not known.*

As concerns tobacco, there are many superstitions. And the chiefest is this—that there is a standard governing the matter, whereas there is nothing of the kind. Each man's own preference is the only standard for him, the only one which he can accept, the only one which can command him. A congress of all the tobacco-lovers in the world could not elect a standard which would be binding upon you or me, or would even much influence us.

The next superstition is that a man has a standard of his own. He hasn't. He thinks he has, but he hasn't. He thinks he can tell what he regards as a good cigar from what he regards as a bad one—but he can't. He goes by the brand, yet imag-

Samuel L. Clemens, *What Is Man? and Other Essays.* New York: Harper and Brothers, 1917.

ines he goes by the flavor. One may palm off the worst counterfeit upon him; if it bears his brand he will smoke it contentedly and never suspect.

Children of twenty-five, who have seven years experience, try to tell me what is a good cigar and what isn't. Me, who never learned to smoke, but always smoked; me, who came into the world asking for a light.

No one can tell me what is a good cigar—for me. I am the only judge. People who claim to know say that I smoke the worst cigars in the world. They bring their own cigars when they come to my house. They betray an unmanly terror when I offer them a cigar; they tell lies and hurry away to meet engagements which they have not made when they are threatened with the hospitalities of my [cigar] box. Now then, observe what superstition, assisted by a man's reputation, can do. I was to have twelve personal friends to supper one night. One of them was as notorious for costly and elegant cigars as I was for cheap and devilish ones. I called at his house and when no one was looking borrowed a double handful of his very choicest; cigars which cost him forty cents apiece and bore red-and-gold labels in sign of their nobility. I removed the labels and put the cigars into a box with my favorite brand on it—a brand which those people all knew, and which cowed them as men are cowed by an epidemic. They took these cigars when offered at the end of the supper, and lit them and sternly struggled with them—in dreary silence, for hilarity died when the fell brand came into view and started around— but their fortitude held for a short time only; then they made excuses and filed out, treading on one another's heels with indecent eagerness; and in the morning when I went out to observe results the cigars lay all between the front door and the gate. All except one—that one lay in the plate of the man from whom I had cabbaged the lot. One or two whiffs was all he could stand. He told me afterward that some day I would get shot for giving people that kind of cigars to smoke.

Mark Twain relaxes with a cigar. Library of Congress

A Discriminating Taste

Am I certain of my own standard? Perfectly; yes, absolutely—unless somebody fools me by putting my brand on some other kind of cigar; for no doubt I am like the rest, and know my cigar by the brand instead of by the flavor. However, my standard is a pretty wide one and covers a good deal of territory. To me, almost any cigar is good that nobody else will smoke, and to me almost all cigars are bad that other people consider good. Nearly any cigar will do me, except a Havana.

People think they hurt my feelings when then come to my house with their life preservers on—I mean, with their own cigars in their pockets. It is an error; I take care of myself in a similar way. When I go into danger—that is, into rich people's houses, where, in the nature of things, they will have high-tariff cigars, red-and-gilt girded and nested in a rosewood box along with a damp sponge, cigars which develop a dismal black ash and burn down the side and smell, and will grow hot to the fingers, and will go on growing hotter and hotter, and go on smelling more and more infamously and unendurably the deeper the fire tunnels down inside below the thimbleful of honest tobacco that is in the front end, the furnisher of it praising it all the time and telling you how much the deadly thing cost—yes, when I go into that sort of peril I carry my own defense along; I carry my own brand—twenty-seven cents a barrel—and I live to see my family again. I may seem to light his red-gartered cigar, but that is only for courtesy's sake; I smuggle it into my pocket for the poor, of whom I know many, and light one of my own; and while he praises it I join in, but when he says it cost forty-five cents I say nothing, for I know better.

However, to say true, my tastes are so catholic [wide-ranging] that I have never seen any cigars that I really could not smoke, except those that cost a dollar apiece. I have examined those and know that they are made of dog-hair, and not good dog-hair at that.

European Influence

I have a thoroughly satisfactory time in Europe, for all over the Continent one finds cigars which not even the most hardened newsboys in New York would smoke. I brought cigars with me, the last time; I will not do that any more. In Italy, as in France, the Government is the only cigar-peddler. Italy has three or four domestic brands: the Minghetti, the Trabuco, the Virginia, and a very coarse one which is a modification of the

Virginia. The Minghettis are large and comely, and cost three dollars and sixty cents a hundred; I can smoke a hundred in seven days and enjoy every one of them. The Trabucos suit me, too; I don't remember the price. But one has to learn to like the Virginia, nobody is born friendly to it. It looks like a rat-tail file, but smokes better, some think. It has a straw through it; you pull this out, and it leaves a flue, otherwise there would be no draught, not even as much as there is to a nail. Some prefer a nail at first. However, I like all the French, Swiss, German, and Italian domestic cigars, and have never cared to inquire what they are made of; and nobody would know, anyhow, perhaps. There is even a brand of European smoking-tobacco that I like. It is a brand used by the Italian peasants. It is loose and dry and black, and looks like tea-grounds. When the fire is applied it expands, and climbs up and towers above the pipe, and presently tumbles off inside of one's vest. The tobacco itself is cheap, but it raises the insurance. It is as I remarked in the beginning—the taste for tobacco is a matter of superstition. There are no standards—no real standards. Each man's preference is the only standard for him, the only one which he can accept, the only one which can command him.

To My Cigar

First published in a book of gentlemen's poetry, this light nineteenth-century poem praises the beauty and comfort of cigar smoking.

Yes, social friend, I love thee well,
  In learned doctor's spite;
thy clouds all other clouds dispel,
  And lap me in delight.
What though they tell, with phizzes
[faces] long,
  My years are sooner past!

I would reply with reason strong,
  They're sweeter while they last.
When in the lonely evening hour,
  Attended but by thee,
O'er history's varied page I pore,
  Man's fate in thine I see.
Oft as the snowy column grows,
  Then breaks and falls away,
I trace how mighty realms thus
rose,
  Thus tumbled to decay.
Awhile like thee earth's masters
burn
  And smoke and fume around;
And then, like thee, to ashes turn,
  And mingle with the ground.
Life's but a leaf adroitly rolled,
  And Time's the wasting breath
That, late or early, we behold
  Gives all to dusty death.
From beggar's frieze [coarse cloth]
to monarch's robe,
  One common doom is passed;
Sweet Nature's works, the swelling
globe,
  Must all burn out at last.
And what is he who smokes thee
now?
  A little moving heap,
That soon, like thee, to fate must
bow,
  With thee in dust must sleep.
But though thy ashes downward
go,

Thy essence rolls on high;
Thus, when my body lieth low,
My soul shall cleave the sky.

Charles Sprague, "To My Cigar,"
in Pipe and Pouch:
The Smoker's Own Book of Poetry.
Boston: Joseph Knight, 1895.

CHAPTER 2

The Cigarette and the Growth of the Smoking Industry, 1900–1960

The Dangers of Smoking

Herbert H. Tidswell

As a practicing doctor in the late nineteenth and early twentieth century, Herbert H. Tidswell was well respected in his field. In his 1912 book The Tobacco Habit, *which is extracted in the following selection, he rails against the dangers of smoking. In an era when the habit was little considered, much less criticized, Tidswell was vehement in his opposition to all forms of tobacco—including the cigarette, which was rapidly becoming popular. The doctor maintains that smoking causes respiratory distress and disease, loss of appetite, and loss of energy—claims that modern medicine has shown to be true. The doctor also points out the detrimental effects of living in a house with smokers. Although the dangers of secondhand smoke are well known in the twenty-first century, in 1912 Tidswell was making a groundbreaking observation.*

I still rejoice at my own liberation from the delusion that tobacco is a panacea for all the ills of life. I am convinced that smoking is a hindrance to the full enjoyment and exercise of the faculties of mind and body. What is the verdict of many an honest smoker? I have heard many smokers express deep regret at being slaves to the habit, confessing its uselessness and its expense, and other drawbacks.

Tobacco tends to make the bread-winner dull of intellect, disinclined for hard work, feeble of digestion, short-winded, short-sighted, dry in the throat, and often thirsting for intoxicating drink. So the unfortunate man has to supply his craving for tobacco and drink before he satisfy the claim of his wife and children. The wife and children are deprived of necessary food and clothing and become feeble and debilitated, if not actually victims to disease.

Herbert H. Tidswell, *The Tobacco Habit: Its History and Pathology: A Study in Birth Rates: Smokers Compared with Non-Smokers.* London: J.&A. Churchill, 1912.

We cannot eradicate disease entirely, but we acknowledge that a great many diseases are preventable, and certainly those which are induced by tobacco and alcohol are preventable.

The medical profession has, at last, roused itself to warn the public about the dangers of excessive drinking, and at last it recognises that the value of alcohol as medicine has been greatly over-rated—the cause of truth advances slowly in our country, because we are so disinclined to think for ourselves and to break through old customs. Is it not our duty to help the rising generation to grow up strong and healthy and free from narcotic taint? Is not hygiene a neglected science amongst the rich and poor? Books on hygiene do not recommend the use of tobacco even in moderation.

Support from the Medical Community

The evils of tobacco inebriety are truthfully described by Dr. Crothers in his work on "*Morphinism and Narcomanias from Other Drugs*," ... he writes thus:

> The tobacco addiction is usually associated with alcohol or other drugs, hence the tobacco disability is seldom considered. In reality, tobacco is a narcotic poison, and its use is not only dangerous, but it is certain to be followed with debility, mental perversion and exhaustion. Statistics show that students and brain workers who use tobacco have less vigour, both mental and physical, and are more liable to disease.

I maintain that the education of a medical man is not complete if he fails to realize the harm of smoking. The subject should be taught in all medical schools as a part of the curriculum. It is unreasonable to expect greater knowledge among the laity [the general public] than medical men. We must lead the way, teach the truth, and show our consistency by acting up to our knowledge. Who can deny the truth of the evidence contained in the pages of *The Lancet* [British medical journal] which I have quoted? The fact that a few men can smoke without harmful consequences, does not prove that it is beneficial to them. No man is justified in playing with poison. I am convinced that the smoker has less resisting power to disease than others.

My opinion is corroborated by the results of the experiments of [zoologist and bacteriologist Élie] Metchnikoff [1845–1916], who has discovered that the white corpuscles of the blood, which he calls phagocytes, eat up intrusive bacteria and other germs, and are the chief means in warding off disease; so that the man or animal who has the normal quantity of healthy active phagocytes is immune, that is to say, he cannot be effectively attacked by disease germs.

Metchnikoff's conclusion is that the phagocytes in our bodies should be stimulated in their activity, in order to successfully fight the germs of infection. He states that alcohol, opium, and quinine hinder the phagocytic action. He does not refer to tobacco, as far as I know, but he declares that opium hinders the activity of the phagocytes. For all we know to the contrary, tobacco may be extremely fatal to them. We depend for immunity, from the attacks of disease germs, on the efficiency of our phagocytes; they form the first line of defence, therefore it is the height of folly, and almost suicidal, to impair their efficiency.

What about the old belief that smoking was a safeguard against infection? It was based on a want of knowledge, and it was a capital excuse for those who liked tobacco. The light of scientific investigation has come to our help, and clearly indicates the dangers of tobacco and other narcotics in rendering the phagocytes inefficient for their physiological functions. We owe a debt of gratitude to Metchnikoff for his discoveries. There is now no excuse for using tobacco, except for simple indulgence, as a form of mental intoxication. Whether it is dear at the price is a matter of opinion. *Chacun à son goût* [Each has his own taste].

A Call to the Community

This consideration opens up an important question for medical officers in the army and navy. Ought they not to avoid smoking, and teach their men to do the same? It is a serious question and demands instant attention.

We want an efficient army and navy to protect our country, our colonies, our Indian empire and our commerce.

We need efficient, clear-headed, far-seeing statesmen and legislators to govern wisely.

We need ministers of religion to set an example of the Christian life, and to show us the advantage of leading a "godly, righteous, and sober life."

We need medical men who will live up to the spirit of the ancient [Greek physician] Hippocrates, and warn their patients against "anything harmful and mischievous."

We need parents and teachers to persuade boys, girls, young men and women to avoid the smoking mania.

We need a long pull, a strong pull, and a pull all together, to save the rising generation from falling victims to a big snare and delusion.

Does smoking promote frivolity of mind? I think no one will deny that the present generation is frivolous. It may appear absurd to connect this phase of character with tobacco, but I know from my personal experience that my own character underwent an extraordinary change under the influence of tobacco. I account for it in this way:

> One of the known effects of tobacco is to cause forgetfulness, especially of higher things.

A dreamy reverie takes the place of manly activity. The discipline and simplicity of early days is forgotten in the clouds of tobacco, and the man who was once in serious earnest in his work may become frivolous, capricious and lethargic.

Look at the countries of Europe now, mostly absorbed in frivolous amusements, and doing little to help the oppressed, or to relieve the sufferings of humanity. The whole body is sick, but the frivolous take no heed. "Let us eat and drink and smoke and enjoy ourselves" is the guiding principle of the multitude. Frivolity must be considered a disease of the mind. We want healthy minds and bodies, and I ask how can one reasonably expect to be strong, vigorous, and contented who perpetually imbibe a narcotic poison which stupifies the brain? I am quite certain that smoking does cause forgetfulness and stupidity, and I am of opinion that many serious accidents are the result of temporary oblivion, the immediate result of narcotic poison. Seeing that tobacco obscures the reason and the intellectual powers, it may be answerable for the want of chivalry, and the want of religion, which we deplore among the Christian nations of Europe and America. It is obvious that forgetfulness is a common result of smoking. I notice it every day of my life. The young men who are smokers are most forgetful, even in the ordinary affairs of business. Many notes of warning have been recently uttered by thoughtful men of various schools, but the people heed them not. The only remedy is to teach the rising generation to abstain from tobacco.

Personal Experiences

I dread touching on this subject, for I consider that the day when I began to smoke was the most unfortunate day in my whole life. I have often testified to the injurious effect it had on me, morally, mentally and physically. I broke myself of the habit finally, with great difficulty, many years ago, and I would not take it up again if I were offered untold wealth to do so. I decline to describe the sufferings I endured, and the painful struggles of conscience; it is enough for me to say that I am fully convinced that tobacco can become a quencher of the Holy Spirit in a man. I may mention one of the ill effects I experienced from tobacco, viz. [namely], occasional loss of sleep after smoking a cigar; only those who have been deprived of a good night's sleep can appreciate its value. Natural sleep is the most precious medicine Nature can give. Art can supply no substitute. This proves that tobacco has a disturbing or exciting action on the brain, resulting from the weak action of the heart, and not to the direct action of tobacco on the nerve cells of the brain.

Insomnia is one of the evils of the day, and is often the result of excessive brain work and anxiety. Can tobacco be recommended as an antidote for a weary, overworked brain? My prescription would be—rest, and food, and fresh air, together with entire abstinence from alcohol and tobacco.

How does tobacco affect a married man in his home? Under the influence of tobacco he becomes lazy, and disinclined for any exertion. He is tempted to shirk many little domestic duties which he might perform, but he hopes his wife will save him all trouble and let him enjoy his reverie. He is no comfort to his wife, and she gets little sympathy from him. Her life becomes one long dreary never-ending task; if sickness attacks the children, all the responsibility is thrust on her shoulders; if the husband is out of work, the wife must go out as a charwoman [a cleaning woman] to provide bread for the husband and children. The willing horse does all the work, but she must be a strong woman if her health will stand such a heavy strain. I think this is no exceptional case: I see so many pale, haggard, thin, care-worn, wrinkled, and yet young women, and I wonder what are the causes, and I think I have pointed out one, at least. Not only is the poor wife overworked all day, but she is liable to be poisoned by night by the exhalations of nicotine which rise from the skin and the lungs of her husband. Then she has headache, faintness, and giddiness, but no one suspects these are the symptoms of nicotine poisoning! The true causes of such symptoms are never suspected.

It is nobody's business to trace disease to its original causes, unless the general practitioner undertakes it. As a rule he has little time for such an enquiry, or feels that it is useless.

Destroyer of Mind and Body

I have heard medical men argue that smoking cannot be one of the chief causes of insanity because the asylums have more female inmates than male. I ask if it is unreasonable to suggest that the gross and brutal selfishness on the part of a husband is not calculated to cause insanity in the wife? Nothing is more difficult than to trace mental disease or insanity to its true origin; there is, however, only too much evidence to show that excessive smoking has often caused insanity. Experience teaches that the mental condition of a husband influences that of his wife: if he is cheerful, hopeful and contented, it helps the wife to be like him; on the other hand, when the husband is morose, dull, idle, or fond of drink and tobacco, he exerts a bad influence over the wife. Hence, the husband who abuses himself with tobacco and alcohol will ultimately destroy his wife's health and happiness. An unhealthy woman is unable to rear healthy children, even in a good environment, and this, I believe, is the explanation of the excessive amount of disease amongst the children of the rich and poor in the countries of Great Britain, Europe and America. Sickly children are always peevish and fretful, and when the parents get weary of their crying they give them sweets to pacify them. A craving for sweets is acquired early in life, and prevents the proper nourishment of the child. The sickly and stunted children that now crowd the schools of this country are a source of grave anxiety to all thoughtful people.

The report of the Inter-Departmental Committee on Physical Deterioration contains ample evidence of the widespread evil of alcoholic excess among men and women, both as a cause of disease and poverty. The evils of juvenile smoking in checking growth were emphasized by Professor Cunningham, but no inquiries were made as to the evils of excessive smoking among adults. This is a serious omission, as superficial observers are apt to conclude that smoking is a harmless pastime. In my opinion it is a dangerous habit for a youth under twenty-one, and is liable to lead to gambling, drinking and other vices.

It always seems illogical to suggest or assert that smoking is harmful before the age of twenty-one, and harmless after that age. I have never received an explanation on this point.

It puzzles me to know how boys will be prevented from smoking and injuring their prospects so long as they see their parents and teachers set such store on it. I was speaking to a man lately, and he said, "smoking is the only pleasure I have in life." Are there not many like him?

Contributor to Poverty

When I was in London . . . I noticed a number of "unemployed" sitting contentedly on the seats and parapets on the Thames Embankment. The majority had their pipes in their mouths and their hands in their pockets, and they did not look eager for work. Now everyone knows that tobacco is not food, but the craving for a smoke is so strong in some men that they are content to starve their stomachs in order to satisfy the craving for a whiff of poison. Such men soon fall victims to consumption and other diseases.

All observers are agreed that the chief factor in causing disease are overcrowding in small tenements, female factory labour, and want of proper care of infants and children. We must not be content with these statements, but we must inquire how it happens that these people are living under such conditions. Why are they so poor that they cannot afford to pay the rent of a nice cottage?

In too many cases their poverty is caused by their indulgence in tobacco and strong drink. What proof can I give of this statentent? Is there any village or town so poor that it cannot support one or more public houses and many tobacconists? The very poorest districts can pay for these injurious luxuries. The law takes care of the property of youths under twenty-one, and does not allow a minor to have control of his property, he is placed under guardians: why does not the law also take an equal care for the health of his body? The most critical time of a lad's life is just after leaving school; if he forms bad habits then he may never be able to regain his self-respect; he needs guidance, help, and protection till he reaches the age of twenty-one. Do fathers and mothers always realize their responsibilities? and do they behave themselves in such a way as to be entitled to the "honour" which children are commanded by God to give to their parents?

Do parents try and help their children to keep the Fifth Commandment? Can children honour and obey parents who stagger, and fight like demons, when under the influence of drink?

Have we traced the craving for alcohol to its origin? It is not a natural craving, it is acquired. In my experience non-smokers hardly ever become drunkards, while nearly all drunkards are smokers.

I am of opinion that the only way to check intemperance is to persuade the lads of our country to pledge themselves to abstain from tobacco and alcohol until they reach the age of twenty-one. Does this suggestion seem impossible? by no means, if the Christian men and women combine and determine to organize societies all over the country to effect this purpose; the majority of lads will see that it is for their good and gladly give the pledge. I appeal to all those who love and serve our Lord Jesus Christ to help in this work.

Marketing Cigarettes to Women in Pre–World War II Society

Larry Tye

In 1998 journalist Larry Tye wrote The Father of Spin, *an account of the life of Edward Bernays, considered the father of modern public relations. Bernays, a nephew of Austrian founder of psychoanalysis Sigmund Freud, changed the landscape of advertising in the first half of the twentieth century by studying human psychology and then selling products by appealing to people's emotions instead of reason. The following selection by Larry Tye describes Bernays's famous advertising campaign for Lucky Strike cigarettes. According to Tye, Bernays single-handedly changed society's view of women smoking. Previously, smoking in public carried a social stigma for women. Through a series of carefully engineered social events and print advertisements, Bernays made smoking an acceptable and even desirable ladies' habit.*

Tobacco tycoons in the United States scored nearly as stunning a triumph as US troops during World War I. When the United States joined the battle, cigarettes were considered unsavory, if not unmanly; most men preferred cigars, pipes, or chewing tobacco. But cigarettes proved more convenient in the trenches, new blended tobaccos produced a milder product, and Uncle Sam began putting cigarettes in soldiers' rations, with the result that many doughboys changed their smoking habits. Cigarettes were manly things now, the stuff of warriors. And as their use soared, so did profits. All of which convinced cigarette makers that the time was ripe to open a second front, this time targeting females.

Larry Tye, "Selling Smoke," *The Boston Globe,* July 19, 1998, p. 16. Copyright © 1998 by Globe Newspaper Company. Reproduced by permission of the author.

In 1928, just as they were beginning that push, Edward L. Bernays started working for George Washington Hill, the president of the American Tobacco Co., which made America's fastest-growing cigarette brand, Lucky Strike. Hill, Bernays later recalled, "became obsessed by the prospect of winning over the large potential female market for Luckies. 'If I can crack that market, I'll get more than my share of it,' he said to me one day. 'It will be like opening a new gold mine right in our front yard.'"

The quickest way to rally women to his cause, the tobacco man believed, was to zero in on their waistlines. His theory was simple: Slimness was coming into vogue, and cigarettes could be sold as a fat-free way to satisfy hunger. He'd already settled on a slogan—"Reach for a Lucky instead of a sweet"— and to bring it to life, he turned to Bernays.

Bernays Takes Over

It was a wise choice. Bernays didn't invent fashions like the quest for a svelte figure, but at 36 he was already becoming the acknowledged master of accentuating such trends and capitalizing on them. He was the man who, more than any other, put bacon and eggs on breakfast tables, Ivory in soap dishes, and books on bookshelves, and kept Calvin Coolidge in the White House. His tactics differed in each case, but his philosophy remained constant. Hired to sell a product, service, or candidate, he instead sold whole new ways of behaving that, over time, reaped huge rewards for his clients. In so doing, Bernays almost singlehandedly fashioned the art of what has come to be called public relations. And if he sometimes took credit for creating a bit more than he actually did, he is nonetheless widely recognized as the man who fathered the science of spin.

At no time was Bernays's skill at reshaping reality clearer than during his eight-year association with the tobacco tycoon Hill, a relationship that budding PR [public relations] men even today revisit as evidence of their enormous power to influence not only what people buy and how they cast their ballots but even what they believe.

Bernays launched his campaign against sweets with his tried-and-true tactic of enlisting "experts," in this case persuading Nickolas Muray, a photographer friend, to ask other artists to sing the praises of the slim. Magazines and newspapers were furnished with the latest findings on the get-thin trend: photo after photo of slender Parisian models in haute couture dresses or medical testimonials warning that sweets caused tooth decay. Bernays even persuaded dancing-school entrepreneur Arthur Murray to sign a letter testifying that "Dancers today, when tempted to overindulge at the punch bowl or the buffet, reach for a cigarette instead."

Cracking the Female Market

Not content to rely on the press or on the influence of experts, Bernays also worked directly to change the way people ate. Hotels were urged to add cigarettes to their dessert lists, while the Bernays office widely distributed a series of menus designed to "save you from the dangers of overeating." They suggested a sensible mix of vegetables, meats, and carbohydrates, followed by the advice to "reach for a cigarette instead of dessert."

The sugar companies and other industries weren't amused. Hill got angry letters from cocoa brokers and peanut-butter makers, from the manufacturers of salted nuts and candy, including one who charged that American Tobacco's attacks were "unfair, unsportsmanlike and absolutely avaricious." And US Senator Reed Smoot, of Utah, a big sugar-beet state, struck back from the Senate floor, calling the tobacco-company campaign an "orgy of buncombe, quackery, and downright falsehood and fraud."

Bernays responded by casting the controversy in the favorable glow of what he called the "new competition." He realized that controversy breeds press coverage, which almost always was good for his client. All this seemed to delight Hill, who wrote to Bernays, "I think the record shows that we have 'shut them up' pretty well." Hill loved the way Bernays used the anti-sweets campaign to promote Luckies, but that only whetted his appetite to crack the female market. Though the share of cigarettes consumed by women more than doubled from 1923 to 1929, it was still just 12 percent. So, early in 1929, Hill summoned Bernays and demanded: "How can we get women to smoke on the street? They're smoking indoors. But, damn it, if they spend half the time outdoors and we can get 'em to smoke outdoors, we'll damn near double our female market. Do something. Act."

Bernays understood that they were up against a social taboo that cast doubt on the character of women who smoked, but he wasn't sure how this stricture could be overcome. So he got Hill to pay for a consultation with Dr. A.A. Brill, a psychoanalyst and a disciple of Bernays's uncle, Dr. Sigmund Freud.

"It's perfectly normal for women to want to smoke cigarettes," Brill advised. "The emancipation of women has suppressed many of their feminine desires. More women now do the same work as men do. . . . Cigarettes, which are equated with men, become torches of freedom."

That rang a bell for Bernays. Why not organize a parade of prominent women lighting their "torches of freedom"? And do it on Easter Sunday, on Fifth Avenue, America's most prestigious promenade?

Breaking of a Taboo

He gathered a list of 30 debutantes from a friend at *Vogue* magazine, then sent each of them a telegram signed by his secretary, Bertha Hunt. "In the interests of equality of the sexes and to fight another sex taboo," the dispatch explained, "I and other young women will light another torch of freedom by smoking cigarettes while strolling on Fifth Avenue Easter Sunday."

A woman poses with a cigarette in this 1920s photo. Advertising in the 1920s and 1930s depicted smoking as glamorous and liberating for women. Library of Congress

The script for the parade was outlined in a memo from Bernays's office. The object, it explained, would be to generate "stories that for the first time women have smoked openly on the streets. These will take care of themselves, as legitimate news, if the staging is rightly done. Undoubtedly after the stories and pictures have appeared, there will be protests from nonsmokers and believers in 'Heaven, home and mother.' These should be watched for and answered in the same papers."

What kind of marchers would be best? "Because it should appear as news with no division of the publicity, actresses should be definitely out. . . . Of course," the memo advised, the debutantes "are not to smoke simply as they come down the church steps. They are to join in the Easter parade, puffing away."

The actual march went off more smoothly than even its scriptwriters imagined. Ten young women turned out, marching down Fifth Avenue with their lighted "torches of freedom," and the newspapers loved it. Photographs showed elegant ladies, with floppy hats and fur-trimmed coats, cigarettes held self-consciously by their sides, as they paraded down the wide boulevard. Dispatches ran the next day, generally on Page 1, in papers from Fremont, Nebraska, to Portland, Oregon, to Albuquerque, New Mexico. During the following days, women were reported to be taking to the streets, cigarettes in hand, in Boston and Detroit, Wheeling, West Virginia, and San Francisco. Women's clubs, meanwhile, were enraged about these forward females, and for weeks afterward, editorial writers churned out withering prose, pro and con.

The uproar he had touched off proved enlightening to Bernays. "Age-old customs, I learned, could be broken down by a dramatic appeal, disseminated by the network of media," he wrote in his memoirs. "Of course the taboo was not destroyed completely. But a beginning had been made."

How Much Did Bernays Know?

The Torches of Freedom campaign remains a classic in the world of public relations, one still cited in classrooms and boardrooms. Yet there's another, more troubling side to the story of Bernays's bid to get women smoking, one not discussed in his 849-page autobiography and never mentioned in his countless tellings and retellings of the American Tobacco tale over the subsequent 66 years.

For starters, Bernays almost always concealed the fact that American Tobacco was behind his motives. Discerning readers might have suspected that a commercial interest had prompted the campaign, but it would have taken a detective to pinpoint the company. To be fair, there's disagreement in the public relations community even today about the propriety of masking a client's identity, and there was far less consensus when Bernays was working for American Tobacco. Yet, in many an interview, Bernays maintained that his own standards were beyond reproach, such as when he told a public relations historian in 1959 that whenever his firm enlisted experts, "we did it in an open and overt way."

If he began by disguising his role in the battle to get women smoking, Bernays more than made up for that in later years. The parade story in particular became part of his repertoire on the speaking circuit and in the scores of interviews he granted before his death, in 1995. With each retelling, the tale got more colorful and his claims more sweeping. In his 1965 memoirs, for instance, Bernays discussed the slow process of breaking down conventions, like the taboo against women smoking. By 1971 he was telling an oral historian at Columbia University that "overnight the taboo was broken by one overt act."

Beyond his apparent embellishment, however, is the more vexing question of how much he knew back then about the risks of smoking. His papers and those of American Tobacco make clear that company executives were beginning to sense how hazardous tobacco products could be, and that Bernays was becoming their point man in deflating those dangers. And even as he was peddling cigarettes to American women, he was doing all he could to persuade his wife, Doris, to give up her pack-a-day habit.

"He used to hide my mother's cigarettes and make us hide the cigarettes. He didn't think they were good for Mother," remembers his elder daughter, also named Doris. Anne, his younger daughter, recalls that when her father found a pack of her mother's Parliaments, "he'd pull them all out and just snap them like bones, just snap them in half and throw them in the toilet. He hated her smoking." Whatever his attitude at home, at work Bernays had to serve the swashbuckling Hill. And in 1934, Hill was worried about new surveys showing that many women wouldn't smoke Luckies because the package, green with a red bull's-eye, clashed with their favorite clothing. "What do you suggest?" Bernays remembered Hill asking. The PR man replied, "Change the Lucky package to a neutral color that will match anything they wear." That was all Hill needed to set him off: "I've spent millions of dollars advertising the package. Now you ask me to change it."

Lucky Strike and the Green Ball

First, he analyzed the color itself. A book entitled *The Language of Color* told him that green was an "emblem of hope, victory, and plenty" and "symbolical of solitude and peace"—upbeat themes to build on. Even more encouraging were statistics showing that green already made up about 20 percent of the current lines being turned out by French fashion houses.

What Bernays needed was a big event to light up the world of fashion. He settled on a Green Ball, to be held at the stately Waldorf-Astoria [hotel] and attended by New York's leading debutantes, with proceeds going to some deserving charity. And he found the ideal hostess: Mrs. Frank A. Vanderlip, chairwoman of the Women's Infirmary of New York and wife of the former chairman of the National City Bank.

All Mrs. Vanderlip needed to know, Bernays decided, was that proceeds would buy milk for undernourished kids, furnish clothing to cardiac patients, and support other projects at the infirmary. "I explained," he wrote later, "that a nameless sponsor would defray the costs up to $25,000; our client would donate our services to promote the ball; the color green would be the ball's motif and the obligatory color of all the gowns worn at the ball."

The fashion and accessories industries were his next targets. A Green Ball would require not just green gowns but also, Bernays insisted, green gloves and green shoes, green handkerchiefs, and, yes, green jewelry. He began by approaching the Onondaga Silk Co., filling in its president, Philip Vogelman, on plans for the ball and suggesting that he could be at the leading edge of the move to green—if he moved fast.

Vogelman signed up, and he invited fashion editors to the Waldorf for a Green Fashions Fall Luncheon with, of course, green-tinted menus featuring green beans, asparagus-tip salad, broiled French lamb chops with haricots verts and olivette potatoes, pistachio mousse glace, green mints, and creme de menthe. The head of the Hunter College art department gave a talk, "Green in the Work of Great Artists," and a psychologist spoke on the psychological implications of green. The press took note, with the *New York Sun* declaring, "It Looks Like a Green Winter."

Repetition as a Marketing Strategy

But what if the new green clothing clashed with people's decor? A Color Fashion Bureau, under the auspices of Onondaga Silk, was there with advice, sending 1,500 letters on the up-and-coming color to interior decorators, home-furnishings buyers, art-industry groups, and clubwomen. The bureau also sent 5,000 announcements to department stores and merchandise managers.

By now, the bandwagon seemed to be rolling on its own. Mrs. Vanderlip enlisted for her invitation committee luminaries like Mrs. James Roosevelt, Mrs. Walter Chrysler, Mrs. Irving Berlin, and Mrs. Averell Harriman. Altman's and Bonwit Teller filled their Fifth Avenue windows with green gowns, suits, and accessories, and Vogue ran two pages of sketches of the green dresses to be brought to New York from Paris. Bernays was particularly delighted when the "unsuspecting opposition gave us a boost: the November magazine advertisements for Camel cigarettes showed a girl wearing a green dress with red trimmings, the colors of the Lucky Strike package. The advertising agency had chosen green because it was now the fashionable color."

The lesson, Bernays wrote years afterward, is that "emphasis by repetition gains acceptance for an idea, particularly if the repetition comes from different sources."

The Green Ball came off as planned, maybe better. It was a "gay, vivid night, something to remember," Vogue reported. In the same issue: "We thought the lovely ladies who were all done up in green to take part in the pageant of paintings looked unusually lovely." And then this: "The Waldorf did the graceful thing, as usual, and put a flourishing finish on The Green Ball last week by setting a Continental boîte de nuit [night club]. They called it the Casino Vert [green] and carried out the colour motif of the ball by flooding the crystal chandeliers and the mirrored walls with a green-blue light."

But did Hill, who attended the ball, think it and accompanying campaign benefited him and Lucky Strike?

Bernays said the tobacco tycoon seldom offered praise, and in the case of The Green Ball, "I don't recall bothering to check Hill's reaction." Still, he added, "the color green was so omnipresent that he could not escape it. . . . The ball firmly established green's predominance."

Other, more neutral observers disagree over the success of the green campaign. Edwin P. Hoyt, in his book The Super-

salesmen says the whole episode was a great example of the "phenomenal mistakes" that Hill made during his career. "He wanted to establish green that year as the color for women's fashions. He failed dismally." But 16 years later, author Robert Sobel reached a decidedly different conclusion: "Green did become the 'in color' that year. Hill was pleased. Bernays received a bonus." Edward L. Bernays, who was known as the "father of public relations," opened his first PR office, in Manhattan, in 1919. His trademark flair—and a propensity for controversy—was to serve him well throughout a career that lasted until he died, in 1995, at the age of 103.

The Antismoking Campaign of the Nazis

Robert N. Proctor

Robert N. Proctor is a professor of the history of science at Stanford University. He has written extensively about health and the Nazi regime in his 1999 book The Nazi War on Cancer. *In this article Proctor offers a startling view of the Nazis as the developers of a successful antismoking campaign, bent on preserving the health of German citizens. The party systematically set about eradicating smoking entirely, by levying and raising cigarette taxes, banning smoking in public places, and restricting tobacco advertising. Proctor also points out the Nazis' understanding of the link between tobacco use and lung cancer was extremely advanced for the era.*

Historians and epidemiologists have only recently begun to explore the Nazi anti-tobacco movement. Germany had the world's strongest antismoking movement in the 1930s and early 1940s, encompassing bans on smoking in public spaces, bans on advertising, restrictions on tobacco rations for women, and the world's most refined tobacco epidemiology, linking tobacco use with the already evident epidemic of lung cancer. The anti-tobacco campaign must be understood against the backdrop of the Nazi quest for racial and bodily purity, which also motivated many other public health efforts of the era. . . .

Germany had the world's strongest antismoking movement in the 1930s and early 1940s, supported by Nazi medical and military leaders worried that tobacco might prove a hazard to the race. Many Nazi leaders were vocal opponents of smoking. Anti-tobacco activists pointed out that whereas

Robert N. Proctor, "The Anti-Tobacco Campaign of the Nazis: A Little Known Aspect of Public Health in Germany, 1933–1945," *The British Medical Journal,* vol. 313, December 7, 1996, pp. 1,450–53. Copyright © 1996 by the British Medical Association. Reproduced by permission of the BMJ Publishing Group.

[Winston] Churchill, [Joseph] Stalin, and [Franklin] Roosevelt were all fond of tobacco, the three major fascist leaders of Europe—[Adolf] Hitler, [Benito] Mussolini, and [Francisco] Franco—were all non-smokers. Hitler was the most adamant, characterising tobacco as "the wrath of the Red Man against the White Man for having been given hard liquor." At one point the Fuhrer even suggested that Nazism might never have triumphed in Germany had he not given up smoking.

German smoking rates rose dramatically in the first six years of Nazi rule, suggesting that the propaganda campaign launched during those early years was largely ineffective. German smoking rates rose faster even than those of France, which had a much weaker anti-tobacco campaign. German per capita tobacco use between 1932 and 1939 rose from 570 to 900 cigarettes a year, whereas French tobacco consumption grew from 570 to only 630 cigarettes over the same period.

Smith et al [G.D. Smith, S.A. Strobele, and M. Egger] suggested that smoking may have functioned as a kind of cultural resistance, though it is also important to realise that German tobacco companies exercised a great deal of economic and political power, as they do today. German anti-tobacco activists frequently complained that their efforts were no match for the "American style" advertising campaigns waged by the tobacco industry. German cigarette manufacturers neutralised early criticism—for example, from the SA (Sturm-Abteilung; stormtroops), which manufactured its own "Sturmzigaretten" [storm cigarettes]—by portraying themselves as early and eager supporters of the regime. The tobacco industry also launched several new journals aimed at countering anti-tobacco propaganda. In a pattern that would become familiar in the United States and elsewhere after the second world war, several of these journals tried to dismiss the anti-tobacco movement as "fanatic" and "unscientific." One such journal featured the German word for science twice in its title.

We should also realise that tobacco provided an important source of revenue for the national treasury. In 1937–8 German national income from tobacco taxes and tariffs exceeded 1 billion Reichsmarks [German currency]. By 1941, as a result of new taxes and the annexation of Austria and Bohemia, Germans were paying nearly twice that. According to Germany's national accounting office, by 1941 tobacco taxes constituted about one twelfth of the government's entire income. Two hundred thousand Germans were said to owe their livelihood to tobacco—an argument that was reversed by those who pointed to Germany's need for additional men in its labour force, men who could presumably be supplied from the tobacco industry.

Culmination of the Campaign: 1939–41

German anti-tobacco policies accelerated towards the end of the 1930s, and by the early war years tobacco use had begun to decline. The Luftwaffe [air force] banned smoking in 1938 and the post office did likewise. Smoking was barred in many workplaces, government offices, hospitals, and rest homes. The NSDAP (Nationalsozialistische Deutsche Arbeiterpartei) [National Socialist German Labor Party] announced a ban on smoking in its offices in 1939, at which time SS chief Heinrich Himmler announced a smoking ban for all uniformed police and SS officers while on duty. The *Journal of the American Medical Association* that year reported [founder of the Gestapo, the German political police force] Hermann Goering's decree barring soldiers from smoking on the streets, on marches, and on brief off duty periods.

Sixty of Germany's largest cities banned smoking on street cars in 1941. Smoking was banned in air raid shelters—though some shelters reserved separate rooms for smokers. During the war years tobacco rationing coupons were denied to pregnant women (and to all women below the age of 25) while restaurants and cafes were barred from selling cigarettes to female customers. From July 1943 it was illegal for anyone under the age of 18 to smoke in public. Smoking was banned on all German city trains and buses in 1944, the initiative coming from Hitler himself, who was worried about exposure of young female conductors to tobacco smoke. Nazi policies were heralded as marking "the beginning of the end" of tobacco use in Germany.

German tobacco epidemiology by this time was the most advanced in the world. Franz H Muller in 1939 and Eberhard Schairer and Erich Schoniger in 1943 were the first to use case-control epidemiological methods to document the lung cancer hazard from cigarettes. Muller concluded that the "extraordinary rise in tobacco use" was "the single most important cause of the rising incidence of lung cancer." Heart disease was another focus and was not infrequently said to be the most serious illness brought on by smoking. Late in the war nicotine was suspected as a cause of the coronary heart failure suffered by a surprising number of soldiers on the eastern front. A 1944 report by an army field pathologist found that all 32 young soldiers whom he had examined after death from heart attack on the front had been "enthusiastic smokers." The author cited the Freiburg pathologist Franz Buchner's view that cigarettes should be considered "a coronary poison of the first order."

On 20 June 1940 Hitler ordered tobacco rations to be distributed to the military "in a manner that would dissuade" soldiers from smoking. [According to historian W. Kittel] cigarette rations were limited to six per man per day, with alternative rations available for non-smokers (for example, chocolate or extra food). Extra cigarettes were sometimes available for purchase, but these were generally limited to 50 per man per month and were often unavailable—as during times of rapid advance or retreat. Tobacco rations were denied to women accompanying the Wehrmacht [armed forces]. An ordinance on 3 November 1941 raised tobacco taxes to a higher level than they had ever been (80–95% of the retail price). Tobacco taxes would not rise that high again for more than a quarter of a century after Hitler's defeat. . . .

Impact of the War and Postwar Poverty

Postwar poverty further cut consumption. According to official statistics German tobacco use did not reach prewar levels again until the mid-1950s. The collapse was dramatic: German per capita consumption dropped by more than half from 1940 to 1950, whereas American consumption nearly doubled during that period. French consumption also rose, though during the four years of German occupation cigarette consumption declined by even more than in Germany—suggesting that military conquest had a larger effect than Nazi propaganda.

After the war Germany lost its position as home to the world's most aggressive anti-tobacco science. Hitler was dead but also many of his anti-tobacco underlings either had lost their jobs or were otherwise silenced. Karl Astel, head of Jena's Institute for Tobacco Hazards Research (and rector of the University of Jena and an officer in the SS), committed suicide in his office on the night of 3–4 April 1945. Reich Health Fuhrer Leonardo Conti, another anti-tobacco activist, committed suicide on 6 October 1945 in an allied prison while awaiting prosecution for his role in the euthanasia programme. Hans Reiter, the Reich Health Office president who once characterised nicotine as "the greatest enemy of the people's health" and "the number one drag on the German economy" was interned in an American prison camp for two years, after which he worked as a physician in a clinic in Kassel, never again returning to public service. Gauleiter Fritz Sauckel, the guiding light behind Thuringia's antismoking campaign and the man who drafted the grant application for Astel's anti-tobacco institute, was executed on 1 October 1946 for crimes against humanity. It is hardly surprising that much of the wind was taken out of the sails of Germany's anti-tobacco movement.

Smith et al were correct to emphasise the strength of the Nazi antismoking effort and the sophistication of Nazi era tobacco science. The antismoking science and policies of the era have not attracted much attention, possibly because the impulse behind the movement was closely attached to the larger Nazi movement. That does not mean, however, that antismoking movements are inherently fascist: it means simply that scientific memories are often clouded by the celebrations of victors and that the political history of science is occasionally less pleasant than we would wish.

The Cigarette as a Pleasant Pastime

Ernest Dichter

Ernest Dichter has been called the father of motivational research for developing many of the ideas that shaped advertising in the 1940s and 1950s. Dichter focused on using psychoanalytic therapy techniques to analyze the behavior of consumers. In this extract from his 1947 book The Psychology of Everyday Living, *Dichter explains in simple terms that smoking is popular and deep-rooted in American culture because the habit carries with it pleasant associations from childhood. He also argues that Americans view smoking as a relaxing reward for their hard work and a way to relieve frustration. As an advertiser Dichter learned to promote cigarettes by appealing to people's emotional associations with smoking.*

None of the much flaunted appeals of cigarette advertisers, such as superior taste and mildness, induces us to become smokers or to choose one brand in preference to another. Despite the emphasis put on such qualities by advertisers, they are minor considerations. This is one of the first facts we discovered when we asked several hundred people, from all walks of life, why they liked to smoke cigarettes. Smoking is as much a psychological pleasure as it is a physiological satisfaction. As one of our respondents explained: "It is not the taste that counts. It's that sense of satisfaction you get from a cigarette that you can't get from anything else."

Smoking Is Fun

What is the nature of this psychological pleasure? It can be traced to the universal desire for self-expression. None of us ever completely outgrows his childhood. We are constantly

Ernest Dichter, *The Psychology of Everyday Living*. New York: Barnes & Noble, 1947.

hunting for the carefree enjoyment we knew as children. As we grew older, we had to subordinate our pleasures to work and to the necessity for unceasing effort. Smoking, for many of us, then, became a substitute for our early habit of following the whims of the moment; it becomes a legitimate excuse for interrupting work and snatching a moment of pleasure. "You sometimes get tired of working intensely," said an accountant whom we interviewed, "and if you sit back for the length of a cigarette, you feel much fresher afterwards. It's a peculiar thing, but I wouldn't think of just sitting back without a cigarette. I guess a cigarette somehow gives me a good excuse."

Smoking Is a Reward

Most of us are hungry for rewards. We want to be patted on the back. A cigarette is a reward that we can give ourselves as often as we wish. When we have done anything well, for instance, we can congratulate ourselves with a cigarette, which certifies, in effect, that we have been "good boys." We can promise ourselves: "When I have finished this piece of work, when I have written the last page of my report, I'll deserve a little fun. I'll have a cigarette."

The first and the last cigarette in the day are especially significant rewards. The first one, smoked right after breakfast, is a sort of anticipated recompense. The smoker has work to do, and he eases himself into the day's activities as pleasantly as possible. He gives himself a little consolation prize in advance, and at the same time manages to postpone the evil hour when he must begin his hard day's work. The last cigarette of the day is like "closing a door." It is some thing quite definite. One smoker explained: "I nearly always smoke a cigarette before going to bed. That finishes the day. I usually turn the light out after I have smoked the last cigarette, and then turn over to sleep."

Smoking is often merely a conditioned reflex. Certain situations, such as coming out of the subway, beginning and ending work, voluntary and involuntary interruptions of work, feelings of hunger, and many others regulate the timetable of smoking. Often a smoker may not even want a cigarette particularly, but he will see someone else take one and then he feels that he must have one, too.

While to many people smoking is fun, and a reward in itself, it more often accompanies other pleasures. At meals, a cigarette is somewhat like another course. In general, smoking introduces a holiday spirit into everyday living. It rounds out other forms of enjoyment and makes them one hundred per cent satisfactory.

Smoking Is Oral Pleasure

As we have said, to explain the pleasure derived from smoking as taste experience alone, is not sufficient. For one thing, such an explanation leaves out the powerful erotic sensitivity of the oral zone. Oral pleasure is just as fundamental as sexuality and hunger. It functions with full strength from earliest childhood. There is a direct connection between thumbsucking and smoking. "In school I always used to chew a pencil or a pen," said a journalist, in, reply to our questions. "You should have seen the collection I had. They used to be chewed to bits. Whenever I try to stop smoking for a while, I get something to chew on, either a pipe or a menthol cigarette. You just stick it in your mouth and keep on sucking. And I also chew a lot of gum when I want to cut down on smoking. . . ."

The satisfied expression on a smoker's face when he inhales the smoke is ample proof of his sensuous thrill. The immense power of the yearning for a cigarette, especially after an enforced abstinence, is acknowledged by habitual smokers. One of our respondents said: "When you don't get a cigarette for a long time and you are kind of on pins, the first drag goes right down to your heels.". . .

Cigarettes Help Us to Relax

One shortcoming of our modern culture is the universal lack of adequate relaxation. Many of us not only do not know how to relax, but do not take time to learn. Smoking helps us to relax because, like music, it is rhythmic. Smoking gives us a legitimate excuse to linger a little longer after meals, to stop work for a few minutes, to sit at home without doing anything that requires effort. Here is a nostalgic comment contributed by a strong defender of smoking: "After a long day's work, to get home and sit in a chair and stretch my legs 'way out, and then to sit back and just smoke a cigarette and think of nothing, just blow the smoke in the air—that's what I like to do when I have had a pretty tough day." The restful effect of moderate smoking explains why people working under great stress use more tobacco.

In times of high tension, cigarettes provide relief, as indicated by the following typical comments of one of our respondents: "When I have a problem, and it comes back and back, warningly saying, 'Well, what are you going to do about this?' a cigarette almost acts like a consolation. Somehow it relieves the pressure on my chest. The feeling of relief is almost like what you feel in your chest after you have cried because something has hurt you very much. Relaxing is not the right kind of word for that feeling. It is like having been in a stuffy room for a long time and at last getting out for a deep breath of air." That man's explanation comes very close to stating the scientific reason why smoking brings relief. Worry, anxiety, depress us not only psycho logically but also physiologically. When a person feels depressed, the rhythm of his breathing becomes upset. A short and shallow breath creates a heavy feeling in the chest. Smoking may relieve mental depression by forcing a rhythmic expansion of the breast and thus restoring the normal pace of breathing. The "weight on the chest" is removed.

This connection between smoking and respiration accounts for the common expression, "Smoking helps us to let off steam." When we are enraged, we breathe heavily. Smoking makes us breathe more steadily, and thus calms us down. . . .

A Package of Pleasure

A new pack of cigarettes gives one a pleasant feeling. A full, firm pack in the hand signifies that one is provided for, and gives satisfaction, whereas an almost empty pack creates a feeling of want and gives a decidedly unpleasant impression. The empty pack gives us a feeling of real frustration and deprivation.

During the seventeenth century, religious leaders and statesmen in many countries condemned the use of tobacco. Smokers were excommunicated by the Church and some of them were actually condemned to death and executed. But the habit of smoking spread rapidly all over the world. The psychological pleasures derived proved much more powerful than religious, moral, and legal persuasions. As in the case of the prohibition experiment in the United States, repressive measures seem to have aroused a spirit of popular rebellion and helped to increase the use of tobacco.

If we consider all the pleasure and advantages provided, in a most democratic and international fashion, by this little white paper roll, we shall understand why it is difficult to destroy its power by means of warnings, threats, or preachings. This pleasure miracle has so much to offer that we can safely predict the cigarette is here to stay. Our psychological analysis is not intended as a eulogy of the habit of smoking, but rather as an objective report on why people smoke cigarettes. Perhaps this will seem more convincing if we reveal a personal secret: We ourselves do not smoke at all. We may be missing a great deal.

The Rise of Filtered Cigarettes

Susan Wagner

Cigarette Country: Tobacco in American History and Politics by Susan Wagner, an overview of the political and social history of tobacco in the United States, was one of the most influential books of the 1970s. In this extract from the book, Wagner describes how the growing scientific evidence that smoking causes cancer led cigarette manufacturers to develop filtered cigarettes that supposedly reduced the amount of nicotine and tar smokers inhaled. Anxious to bolster declining cigarette sales, the tobacco industry promoted filtered cigarettes as a safer, healthier alternative, Wagner writes. Every cigarette company developed a filtered brand and competed fiercely for market share. By 1960 the Federal Trade Commission banned ads that claimed that filtered cigarettes were safer, which ironically decreased the motivation of tobacco companies to develop more effective filters. Susan Wagner writes for a welfare-to-work program called Project Match.

When the question of smoking and health became a matter of general public discussion in 1953, the industry plunged into a state of ulcerous tension. For the first time in twenty-one years, the upward curve of cigarette sales, impervious to wars and depression, leveled off and declined slightly. Over the two-year period 1953–54, total consumption declined 6.4 per cent and per capita consumption declined 8.8 per cent. While the "Eisenhower boom" sent stock-market prices spiraling to new highs, tobacco shares wavered at previous levels. Publicity attending the mounting evidence of serious health hazards in smoking is the only factor that has ever been suggested to explain these declines.

The situation was sufficiently perturbing to induce the major tobacco manufacturing and handling companies to take full-page display ads in the press at the beginning of 1954. These ads said that while the industry had full confidence that its products were not injurious to health, it was "pledging aid and assistance to the research effort into all phases of tobacco use and health," and had set up a Tobacco Industry Research Committee (TIRC), to be directed by "a scientist of unimpeachable integrity and national repute," which would have available the services of "an Advisory Board of Scientists disinterested in the cigarette industry." The man named scientific director of TIRC—later renamed the Council for Tobacco Research-U.S.A.—was Dr. Clarence Cook Little, an eminent geneticist and cancer specialist, who at the time of his appointment was director of the Roscoe B. Jackson Memorial Laboratory at Bar Harbor, Maine, and who had formerly been managing director of the American Society for Control of Cancer, the predecessor of the American Cancer Society. The TIRC was to sponsor research into questions of tobacco and health and to "communicate authoritative factual information on the subject to the public." The manufacturers were to support this research. This brainchild was delivered by Hill and Knowlton, the resourceful public relations firm of international fame. Although research money was to be awarded with no strings attached, the TIRC nicely served the purpose of identifying the industry with the welfare of humanity and spreading good will through the scientific community.

Unable to Stop the Tide

But bad news continued to come in from the scientific front. After 1954, a great quantity of new research was published, almost all of which tended to show that cigarette-smoking is a causative factor in lung cancer and other diseases. The U.S. Public Health Service (PHS) became officially engaged in an appraisal of the available data on smoking and health in June, 1956, when, at the instigation of the Surgeon General, a scien-

Statement of the Tobacco Industry Research Committee

The tobacco industry reacted to growing reports that smoking causes cancer by forming the Tobacco Industry Research Committee to investigate these claims. The committee released the following statement to over four hundred newspapers on January 4, 1954.

Recent reports on experiments with mice have given wide publicity to a theory that cigarette smoking is in some way linked with lung cancer in human beings.

Although conducted by doctors of professional standing, these experiments are not regarded as conclusive in the field of cancer research. However, we do not believe that any serious medical research, even though its results are inconclusive should be disregarded or lightly dismissed.

At the same time, we feel it is in the public interest to call attention to the fact that eminent doctors and research scientists have publicly questioned the claimed significance of these experiments.

Tobacco Industry Research Committee,
"A Frank Statement to Cigarette Smokers,"
press release, January 4, 1954.
www.tobacco.neu.edu/litigation/cases/
supportdocs/ frank_ad.htm.

tific study group was set up to make a comprehensive review of the evidence. The group, put together by the National Cancer Institute, the National Heart Institute, the American Cancer Society, and the American Heart Association, appraised sixteen independent studies carried on in five countries over a period of eighteen years and concluded that there is a causal relationship between excessive smoking of cigarettes and lung cancer. On March 6, 1957, it issued a report that said: "The evidence of cause-effect relationship is adequate for considering the initiation of public health measures." The British Medical Research Council completed a comprehensive review of the evidence in June, 1957. Its conclusions were similar. And in July, 1957, U.S. Surgeon General Dr. Leroy Burney declared: "The Public Health Service feels the weight of the evidence is increasingly pointing in one direction: that excessive smoking is one of the causative factors in lung cancer." In a special article entitled "Smoking and Lung Cancer—A Statement of the Public Health Service," published in the *Journal of the American Medical Association* on November 28, 1959, Dr. Burney reiterated that belief.

The Industry Attacks

The manufacturers had to do something. The "health scare" led to the revival of the filter cigarette favored by Russian aristocrats and New Yorkers in the old days. The filter brands evolved from the so-called "mouthpiece" cigarette, dating back to the nineteenth century, which had a stiff paper tube extending from the tobacco column containing a tuft of cotton. These filters were not easy to make; such brands as Tolstoi and Svoboda were expensive specialities. The premium-priced Parliament introduced by Benson & Hedges in 1932 had such a mouthpiece. But popular-priced filter brands were very much the exception before the 1950's.

Brown & Williamson had a filter brand, Viceroy, on the market. Sixteen years after its introduction in 1936, it represented less than 8 per cent of B & W sales. But during the 1950's, Viceroy lifted its company out of the marginal category. First on the filter scene at popular prices, Viceroy was the leading filter brand through 1954. In that year, B & W changed the filter from a hollow tube with cotton to a tip of cellulose acetate—a material that quickly became the "normal" filter throughout the industry.

The filter was the principal device used by merchandisers to reassure smokers. By switching to filter-tip cigarettes, smokers could allay their fears while holding onto their habit. Publicity, particularly a 1954 article in *Reader's Digest,* on the Hammond-Horn report gave filters a great sales boost. Kent, the first filter cigarette to be promoted in a big way (it enjoyed a sudden popularity directly attributable to the *Reader's Digest* story), had been put on the market in 1952 at a premium price by Lorillard, which was not doing as well as it wished with Old Gold even the year before trouble started. The function of a filter was presumably to trap condensates, including nicotine and tars from cigarette smoke. The Kent "micronite" filter was said to subject the smoker to 50 per cent less tar and nicotine than the average, contemporary, nonfilter cigarettes. In a clear response to the "health scare," Kent said that its filter "takes out more nicotine and tars than any other leading cigarette—the difference in protection is priceless." But after an initial spurt, sales of Kent proved disappointing. Smokers found it hard to draw smoke through the filter. In 1957, Lorillard found it necessary to change the filter design and more than double the nicotine content of Kents while nearly doubling the tar content.

Filters Are a Success

Filters proved a convenience as well as a presumed safeguard. They eliminated loose tobacco ends and afforded the smoker a firmer purchase between the lips. Since filters were less expensive than the tobacco they replaced, manufacturers were not reluctant to enter the race to create and promote new filter brands. Some manufacturers saw filters as their salvation. Lorillard's competitors went to work developing filters to compete with Kent's. As demand rose, filter brands multiplied.

In 1953, Liggett & Myers brought out L & M, with a "Pure White Miracle Tip of Alpha-Cellulose" described as "just what the doctor ordered." Reynolds put out Winston, which "filters so effectively." American had its cork-tipped, king-size Herbert Tareyton. But it was now given a "new Selective Filter," with "an entirely new concept in cigarette filtration—a filter tip of purified cellulose, incorporating Activated Charcoal, a filtering substance world famous as a purifying agent." Old Golds came out in a filter version. There was now a three-way cigarette split: regular, nonfilter king, and filter. Other splits followed: Kools and Raleighs came out with filters. Then Philip Morris bought out Benson & Hedges to get Parliament and developed a filter cigarette of its own from an old property, Marlboro, which was dressed up with a cellulose acetate filter trade-named "Selectrate" and packed in a hinged "flip-top" or crush-proof box. The "tar derby" was in full swing. Cigarette sales, instead of entering a permanent decline after a two-year drop, moved up again.

The Cigarette Renaissance

By this time, the selling of the cigarette had entered into a new phase. Tobacco manufacturers were pouring more and more money into television advertising. From about $40 million in 1957, they increased spending on TV to about $115 million in 1961. Squads of beautiful girls and virile young men, water skiers, pilots, speedboat racers—you name it—had been let loose on the home screen in the tobacco industry's frenzied efforts to overcome the bad news from medical circles. Brand image was the big thing, and motivational research had become the byword on Madison Avenue. In 1956, the Cigar Institute decided to demasculinize the cigar to appeal to women. Now, with the help of market research, Philip Morris went all out to give Marlboro a male-oriented image. A rugged rancher type who had come up the hard way and got tattooed somewhere along the line, he was the brooding smoker in "Marlboro country."

The FTC's Attack on Cigarette Advertising

By the mid-1950's, cigarette advertising shouted conflicting claims for cigarettes that were low, lower, and lowest in tar and nicotine. The Federal Trade Commission [FTC] had by then chalked up an impressive series of court decisions upholding its right to protect consumers against claims that smoking is somehow beneficial to health or helps weight-reducing. In 1952, the FTC had worked itself into a fury at Liggett & Myers, whose Chesterfield had once been its darling among tobacco advertisers because it contended itself with the simple slogan "They Satisfy." Following lengthy litigation, words like "milder" and "smoother" had been stricken from the cigarette ad man's vocabulary. For nearly a decade, the FTC had battled Chesterfield's competitors, until binding cease-and-desist orders had been nailed down on therapeutic claims. Now, the FTC was outraged to discover that Liggett & Myers was switching to Chesterfield claims prohibited for other companies and went to court to seek a preliminary injunction barring the new ads. But the U.S. District Court for the Southern District of New York denied the injunction. Finally, after six years of litigation, during the course of which an FTC examiner's finding that "milder" and "smoother" were "puffery" was overturned by the five-member commission, Liggett & Myers was also placed under a cease-and-desist order. But in the light of the growing scientific data that questioned the healthfulness of cigarettes, the FTC action seemed puny. Consumption of cigarettes was increasing, especially among young people, and the agency attributed the increase to advertising.

In 1955, the FTC broadened its attack on cigarette advertising. In September of that year, it issued some guides that prohibited either stated or implied medical approval of smoking in general or any cigarette in particular. Unsubstantiated claims about nicotine, tars, or other components were also barred. After the guides were issued, the FTC began to monitor all cigarette advertising. But there were ways to modify ads so as to imply that smoking was a healthful activity without actually saying so. To the chagrin of the FTC, these commercials did not run afoul of the law. A health warning was needed, but in the absence of a government position on the health question, this was not possible. . . .

The Market Continues to Grow

Innovations in filtration continued. "High filtration" was a term adopted in 1957 to mean substantial reduction in delivered smoke solids. But what was the consumer to do? If he followed the cigarette ads as a source of information, he would be, in the words of a January 24, 1958, *Wall Street Journal* article, "utterly confused." "Philip Morris says its new Parliament filter has '30,000 filaments.' Liggett & Myers Tobacco Company's television commercials talk about its L & M miracle tip with United States patent number 2,805,671. To say nothing of Hit Parade's '40,000 filter traps'!"

The tar derby continued unabated. The FTC guides may have had some effect in eliminating health claims from cigarette advertising, but they had little effect on tar and nicotine claims. Filter brands included regular and king sizes as well as mentholated smokes, which had quickly become the fastest-growing segment of the industry after Salem, in 1956, combined a menthol flavoring with a filter tip, and sales began to increase. Mentholated cigarettes were promoted as "cool" or "fresh," and millions of smokers switched. There were sharp increases in expenditures on television advertising for brands such as Newport, Salem, Alpine, Belair. Apparently, many smokers were convinced that filter and menthol-filter cigarettes were less hazardous to health than regular cigarettes. In 1952, only 1.5 per cent of the cigarettes sold in this country had filters. By 1956, filter-tip sales had ballooned to 30 per cent of the market, and by 1958, filter-tip brands rose to 46 per cent of sales. Mentholated brands accounted for about one in every six filter cigarettes smoked and one-twelfth of the total cigarette market. . . .

The "Tar Derby" Draws to a Close

The "filtered fifties" ended on an ironic note. The FTC was still at work [regulating tobacco] but this time the regulatory agency stumbled badly. Efforts to deal with cigarette advertising on a company-by-company basis had proved ineffective. Weary of deciding the legal merits of individual claims, the FTC decided to knock the tar and nicotine out of cigarette advertising altogether. It moved in that direction by sending a letter to manufacturers on December 17, 1959: "We wish to advise that all representations of low or reduced tar or nicotine, whether by filtration or otherwise, will be construed as health claims. . . . Our purpose is to eliminate from cigarette advertising representations which in any way imply health benefit." In 1960, the commission announced that as a result of negotiation with industry, seven major manufacturers had agreed to abandon tar and nicotine claims. FTC Chairman Earl Kintner, an Eisenhower appointee, hailed the action as a landmark in industry-government cooperation.

But the new agreement also suited a powerful element in the industry that had been uneasy about the implied admission of potential harm in smoking involved in the development of filters. The FTC's action to end the "tar derby" had an unintended effect. It lessened incentive to produce a more effective filter. Sales of nonfilter cigarettes stopped their decline. Filters were disparaged in advertising with such innuendos as "Smoking more now but enjoying it less?" Nonfilter cigarettes began to imply safety with such words as "mildness," "gentleness," and "freshness." Pall Mall even claimed that its greater length acted as a sort of filter. The familiar mazes of charts and graphs disappeared from advertising copy, but Parliament promised an "extra margin." Extra margin of what? Safety, of course. To make sure no one missed the message, Parliament ads featured life-preservers, parachutes, a stunt diver's protective padding, and a fencer's mask. Unable to make capital on their relative safety, the high-filtration brands had a struggle just to stay alive. Some dropped out of sight.

CHAPTER 3

Government Efforts to Prevent Nicotine Addiction, 1960–2000

The U.S. Surgeon General's First Report on Smoking

Michael Housman

In the following selection Michael Housman argues that the U.S. surgeon general's report on smoking in 1964 was a turning point in the antismoking movement. In the report Surgeon General Luther Terry stated unequivocally that smoking causes cancer and other health problems. The document had a lasting and profound effect on smoking in America, causing cigarette sales to drop to a level from which they have yet to recover. Housman explains that three factors converged to cause this decline in sales: the influence of the surgeon general, the scientific legitimacy of the report's findings, and the widespread media campaign that accompanied the report. Michael Housman is a doctoral student at the University of Pennsylvania.

On Saturday, January 11, 1964, the U.S. Surgeon General Luther Terry approached the podium of the State Department auditorium to deliver the results of an exhaustive literature review through a 387-page report entitled "Smoking and Health: Report of the Advisory Committee to the Surgeon General of the Public Health Service." There, the government sealed off 200 reporters and the ten members of the Surgeon General's Advisory Committee on Smoking and Health from the rest of the world. Inside the auditorium, Terry offered a two-hour exegesis [explanation] on the report, which amplified the one paramount judgment that "cigarette smoking is a health hazard of sufficient importance in the United States to warrant appropriate remedial action." The committee's report made front-page headlines throughout the country and was

Michael Housman, "Smoking and Health: The 1964 U.S. Surgeon General's Report as a Turning Point in the Antismoking Movement," *Harvard Health Policy Review,* vol. 1, Spring 2001, pp. 118–26. Copyright © 2001 by *Harvard Health Policy Review.* Reproduced by permission of the publisher and the author.

featured prominently on news broadcasts. Nevertheless, the press almost uniformly predicted that while smoking rates might decline in the immediate future, the smoking habit would inevitably prevail and the American public would not permanently change their use of tobacco products. More than thirty years later, smoking rates of American adults have been cut almost in half from 46% to 25% and it appears inevitable that this decline will continue. What caused the media to make such erroneous predictions? What separated this report from the numerous other reports and studies that had been written long before it?

Three major explanations emerge to distinguish this striking phenomenon: (1) the legitimacy, authority, and objectivity of the Surgeon General; (2) the meticulous accumulation and aggregation of scientific evidence that characterized the study; and (3) the widespread campaign that publicized the findings of the report. As a result, despite its rather predictable conclusions, Luther Terry's famous announcement marked an important turning point in the anti-smoking movement, precipitating a decline in smoking that has lasted to the present day.

History and Substance of the Report

In May of 1962, President John F. Kennedy spoke at the very same podium in the State Department auditorium. In response to a question about health hazards attributed to smoking, he responded, "That matter is sensitive enough and the stock market is in sufficient difficulty without my giving you an answer that is not based on complete information, which I don't have." A few weeks later, after examining material gathered by the Public Health Service, Kennedy instructed Terry to go ahead with a plan he had proposed in April to appoint an Advisory Committee on Smoking and Health. After consulting with the tobacco industry, private health organizations, and several federal agencies, Terry picked ten distinguished scientists (who had not taken public positions on the health effects of smoking) to hold nine meetings between November 1962 and December 1963. They reviewed more than 7,000 articles, including 3,000 research reports, and reported its findings two months after Kennedy's assassination.

The Announcement

On Saturday, January 11, 1964, [according to journalist Marjorie Hunter] newsmen, government workers, and tobacco industry spokesmen "puffed self-consciously on cigarettes" in the lobby and corridors outside the State Department auditorium after nine "no smoking" signs had been fastened to the walls inside. Meanwhile, Terry delivered the conclusions of the project for which the principal finding was as follows:

> Cigarette smoking is associated with a 70% increase in the age-specific death rates of males. The total number of excess deaths causally related to cigarette smoking in the U.S. population cannot be accurately estimated. In view of the continuing and mounting evidence from many sources, it is the judgment of the Committee that cigarette smoking contributes substantially to mortality from certain specific diseases and to the overall death rate.

The committee also found that "cigarette smoking is causally related to lung cancer in men; the magnitude of the effect of cigarette smoking far outweighs all other factors. In comparison with non-smokers, average male smokers of cigarettes have approximately a 9- to 10-fold risk of developing lung cancer and heavy smokers at least a 20-fold risk." Additionally, the committee concluded that "cigarette smoking is the most important of the causes of chronic bronchitis in the United States, and increases the risk of dying from chronic bronchitis and emphysema." Furthermore, it "established that male cigarette smokers have a higher death rate from coronary artery disease than non-smoking males." It even went on to state that while the causative role of cigarette smoking in deaths from coronary artery disease had not yet been proven, "the

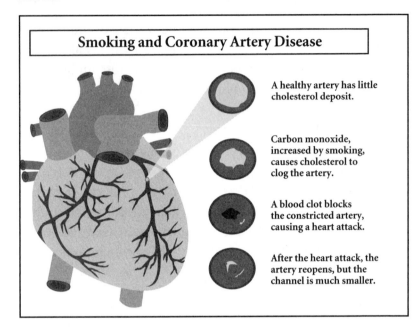

Smoking and Coronary Artery Disease

A healthy artery has little cholesterol deposit.

Carbon monoxide, increased by smoking, causes cholesterol to clog the artery.

A blood clot blocks the constricted artery, causing a heart attack.

After the heart attack, the artery reopens, but the channel is much smaller.

committee considers it more prudent from the public health viewpoint to assume that the established association has causative meaning than to suspend judgment until no uncertainty remains." This statement revealed the rather liberal nature of the committee, which chose to assume a causative role in the absence of more evidence rather than taking a wait-and-see stance. In doing so, the committee implicated cigarette smoking as a leading cause of heart attacks, which was the nation's number one killer at the time (577,000 deaths in 1962). Overall, the report indicted cigarette smoking on a number of different offenses and constituted very bad news for the more than seventy million regular smokers in the U.S. . . .

This Report Was Different

It is clear that the 1964 Surgeon General's report signified some sort of departure from previous work in the field as evidenced by the permanent declines in smoking behavior observed in the decades following its release. While the report alone did not accomplish all of this, it marked the beginning of the most concerted, sustained, and successful effort in history to discourage the use of tobacco. What allowed this report to play such a pivotal role was the convergence of three factors, including the legitimacy and authority of the Surgeon General's office, the meticulous accumulation and aggregation of scientific evidence characterizing the report that resulted in the claim that a "causal" relationship existed, and the widespread campaign that publicized the findings of the report.

While thousands of other studies had been published by individual researchers or partisan organizations such as the American Cancer Society or Council for Tobacco Research (formerly the Tobacco Industry Research Committee), none had the authority, legitimacy or unbiased nature of the U.S. Surgeon General. At the time, few medical authorities were as well respected as the Surgeon General, and Luther Terry's announcement gave the message significant legitimacy by putting the weight of the federal government behind it. . . .

Additionally, a sizeable majority of the reports on smoking and health that were available at the time had either been conducted or funded by openly partisan organizations and the results of such experiments often correlated strongly with the organization that had initiated them. The issue of trust emerged as an obstacle to the ability of Americans to believe how severe the health risks of smoking actually were. However, Luther Terry quite effectively quelled this concern by allowing the creation of the committee to be an open process. [According to the U.S. Public Health Service] the participants "compiled a list of more than 150 scientists and physicians working in the fields of biology and medicine" and "during the next month, these lists were screened by representatives of organizations present at the July 27 [1962] meeting. Any organization could veto any of the names on the list, no reasons being required." Among the representatives in attendance at the July 27 meeting were individuals from all of the major tobacco companies, relevant cancer-related organizations, and government officials. As a result, when the findings from the committee had been published, very few individuals chose to criticize them and even the tobacco companies focused instead upon endorsing Terry's call for "not less but more research." All of these factors allowed the Surgeon General's report to differentiate itself from other studies by establishing the credibility of the source from which the controversial message had come.

The Numbers Hit Home

The Surgeon General's report also involved a methodology that had not been employed before, at least within the United States. Rather than generating its own data, it provided a meticulous accumulation of scientific evidence that considered all points of view and generated a coherent and all-encompassing conclusion. With the help of over 144 consultants, the Surgeon General's Advisory Committee on Smoking and Health was charged with the task of reviewing the 7,000 articles and 3,000 reports that were available on the topic. It also considered statements and pertinent information that other interested parties, particularly the tobacco industry, had submitted to it. These studies had come to similar but nevertheless contradictory conclusions as to the extent of the health hazard that smoking posed. The Surgeon General's report accomplished what most other studies had not in that it synthesized the available literature on the topic and provided a "single, authoritative reading of the mounting evidence" [as scholar Allan M. Brandt writes]. The American people could now reliably state that smoking increased one's chances of dying in any given year by 70% rather than anywhere from 0 to 100% as individual studies may have contended. Additionally, by virtue of its study design, the committee was able to utilize the wide array of sources in order to establish a *causal* relationship between smoking and various illnesses, an association that no other study had been able to reliably accomplish. This achievement was based upon the committee's recognition of the "multiple etiology of biological processes." . . .

Smoking Declines

Though the tobacco industry would continue to dispute this fact to the present day, the ability of the Surgeon General to declare that "cigarette smoking is *causally* related to lung cancer in men" marked an important departure from previous studies which had only been able to demonstrate a strong correlation. The simple use of the word "cause" gave anti-smoking advocates the ammunition they needed to target cigarettes and the tobacco companies as a public health hazard. As a result of this highly effective methodology, the Surgeon General's 1964 report gave the American public a single message equating cigarette smoking with death, thus contributing to the dramatic decline in smoking that was observed immediately after the report was released.

This decline was also the result of a prolonged and widespread publicity campaign that began the instant that the doors to the State Department auditorium were unlocked. As stated previously, the media seized upon this dramatic development that concerned an issue of national importance, and it proceeded to broadcast the words of Luther Terry to all corners of the nation more than it had ever done before. However, the greatest difference between this report and other studies was the fact that various parties made a concerted effort to widely disseminate its conclusions through the use of resources other than the media. One week after Terry's press conference, the Federal Trade Commission [FTC] announced that it planned to require health warnings on every cigarette package and advertisement. Congress superseded FTC action with the Cigarette Labeling and Advertising Act of 1965, which required the warning "Caution: Cigarette Smoking May Be Hazardous to Your Health" on all cigarette packages as of January 1, 1966. Smokers were constantly reminded of the consequences of their habits. Additionally, within a couple years, a major campaign began against smoking as advertisements were placed on billboards, television commercials, and magazines, making the information about the health effects of smoking widely available. As a result, "virtually no one growing up in America since the mid–20th century could seriously claim not to understand—or at least to have heard about—the health risks associated with smoking" [scholar Mark E. Lender notes]. The public had been fully informed of the risks of smoking and was allowed to make its own decision, which undoubtedly contributed to the decline in smoking observed in the decades following Luther Terry's report.

Lasting Effects

Prior to Luther Terry's announcement on the morning of January 11, 1964, almost anyone in the crowd could have guessed what the underlying theme of his speech would be. Ironically enough, once he was finished, almost no one accurately predicted its monumental effects on the smoking habits of Americans. Terry's message was simple as he stated in plain English that "smoking causes cancer" in addition to other health problems. Consequently, cigarette consumption began an immediate and sustained decline which has lasted to the present day as the smoking rate has dropped from 46 to 25%. However, it was not the content of the message but rather its context that separated this report from all others that were available at the time. For the first time, this message was delivered by a well-respected and unbiased medical authority, who reviewed all the available literature on the subject to deliver an all-encompassing statement that was widely publicized to all men, women, and children living in the United States. In these three respects, the Surgeon General's report constituted a remarkable shift from earlier studies and undoubtedly marked the turning point in the anti-smoking movement.

However, its impact upon smoking rates must be understood in a broader context. The importance of the Surgeon General's report on tobacco cannot be under-stated as a contributing factor in the emergence of a policy environment receptive to various tobacco control strategies. While strategies had existed long before the Surgeon General's report, no successful anti-cigarette campaign could be waged before the causal link between smoking and health problems had been established and accepted by the public. The Surgeon General's report filled this role and provided the impetus for a movement that resulted in dramatic changes in smoking and cancer incidence rates.

Cigarette Advertising Should Be Restricted

Ronald G. Vincent

In 1969 Ronald G. Vincent was the associate chief of thoracic surgery at the Roswell Park Memorial Institute in Buffalo, New York. That same year he testified before the U.S. Congress, strongly urging that cigarette advertising be restricted. Such restrictions would protect children from the enticing advertising campaigns designed to addict them to cigarettes at an early age, Vincent argued. In addition, he reiterated the message put forth by the surgeon general in 1964 that smoking causes cancer and death. The tobacco industry cannot be trusted to regulate itself, he asserts, and therefore the federal government must take on that regulatory role. The following selection is an extract of his testimony.

My responsibilities include the diagnosis and treatment of approximately 250 new cases of lung cancer each year. I have no wish to burden these [congressional] Hearings by reiterating the preponderance of scientific data and opinion which has been placed before this [House of Representatives] Committee. Suffice it to say, that less than 10 per cent of these patients with lung cancer will be alive in five years after the establishment of their diagnosis, and more than 96 per cent of them will indicate, for the record, that they smoke a pack or more of cigarettes per day.

My clinical opinion and judgment is that cigarette smoking is a major causal factor in this disease and that if we were able to reduce the amount of smoking done by the population, we would see a proportionate decrease in the amount of lung cancer. It is to be recalled that lung cancer has increased

Ronald G. Vincent, testimony before the U.S. House of Representatives Committee on Interstate and Foreign Commerce, Washington DC: April 18, 1969.

and is continuing to increase in epidemic proportions. Forty years ago it was a clinical nonentity, now it is the leading cause of death by malignant disease in men. There is no evidence that the seriousness of this problem is going to change, unless we either change our smoking habits or the functional design and content of our cigarettes.

Over the past eight years [prior to 1969], I have followed with great interest the deliberations, recommendations and decisions of governmental committees in this particular area of health. I suspect that the historians of the future will look upon our efforts during the past decade with amusement. The record will probably show that here was a highly intellectual society, greatly concerned and oriented toward problems of health, who spent millions of dollars in health research, but with a clearly defined epidemic bursting at their feet, and for reasons of what they thought to be enlightened political and economic self-interest, stood flailing about the branches, while refusing to strike at the roots of the problem.

The Issue Is the Children

As a clinician, who treats smoking-related diseases, I have had the opportunity to discuss this problem with a number of young people, as well as groups of their parents. One question which is always asked is, "Why doesn't the government do something?" I suppose that responsible government officials would reply, "What is there, that is appropriate for the government to do?" Very few would favor prohibition. Certainly, if a man wishes to smoke, he has every right to do so. I feel my responsibility, as a medical clinician, is limited to seeking a means whereby every adult has an opportunity to gain insight into the hazards involved in this particular habit. With the youngsters, however, the situation is quite different.

The youngsters are being systematically enticed by clever and psychologically attractive advertising, to establish a lifelong habit before they reach an age of accountability, and at a time when it is difficult for them to evaluate future consequences in the light of present decisions. The liability of initiating these deceptive policies lies clearly with the tobacco industry. A communications industry, however, that permits, promotes and perpetuates such policies, is not without responsibility. To some, this may seem a rather harsh indictment, but the premise is well established that if you can convince a young person to start smoking, it will take very little to keep him smoking as an adult. I quote from a speech given by a highly respected authority of the tobacco industry:

> So many of our youngsters are heard to say that they have given up smoking in order to buy a motorcycle or a camera or a trip abroad, that one is led to wonder just where lies the point of no return between increasing costs and deteriorating quality. After all, the youngsters' enjoyment of smoking is our future insurance and we ignore their wants at our peril.

As a parent, I, for one, am unwilling to accept the intrusion of this philosophy into my home via the media of television. To be sure, it can be said that the person who does not want to watch cigarette advertising can get up and turn it off, but when you consider that there are fifty-five commercial minutes of cigarette advertising every night on the three major television networks, and that this product is advertised more than any other single product, it would keep a viewer pretty busy trying to avoid it. I, personally, am very reluctant to see restrictions placed upon a communications industry by the government. Most people concerned in this problem have sincerely wished that the broadcasting industry would find it within themselves to institute a form of effective self-regulation with regard to cigarette advertising. Experience in the past five years has shown that this is not, nor will it be, the case. The decision, then, is whether the public desires and recommends limitation of cigarette advertising on television.

Undeniable Evidence

In an attempt to determine the depth of concern of parents, generally, about this problem, a survey was conducted in New York State by 2,000 volunteers of the American Cancer Society. Over 29,000 adults responded to a questionnaire that contained a few very simple and direct inquiries. The result of this survey may be of interest to you and may affect the deliberations of this Committee. 56 per cent of those polled regarded cigarettes as a definite health hazard, while an additional 40 per cent thought they might be, and only 4 per cent thought cigarettes were not a health hazard. 54 per cent were of the opinion that cigarette advertising should be restricted by legislation, while 22 per cent approved current advertising policies, and 24 per cent were unconcerned. 98 per cent were convinced that children should be advised about the hazards of smoking, and that the instructions should come from both the parents and school teachers. Of those who smoked, in the survey, 68 per cent indicated that they would like to stop.

Since the Report of the Surgeon General's Advisory Committee on Smoking and Health in 1964, there have been published over 2,000 research studies, all of which confirm and strengthen the findings of the Surgeon General. Now, even more than in 1964, there is a need for appropriate remedial action.

There is good evidence that the hazard is related to tar yield, and cigarettes can be made less hazardous and in a way that is acceptable to that portion of the public who are unable to stop smoking. Legislation that would progressively reduce the amount of tar yield in cigarettes is desirable. Other remedial action would include making Federal funds available to foster and succor Health Education Programs in schools throughout the Nation. However, in this matter of education, success is not likely to be realized in the presence of unrelenting and overwhelming amounts of cigarette advertising. Advertising which promotes a dubious theme that all that is beautiful and pleasurable in life is associated with cigarette smoking.

A Call to Regulate the Tobacco Industry

There are before you, a number of proposals written in the same verbal tone. They describe themselves as bills "to extend public health protection with respect to cigarette smoking," while at the same time the content of the bills specifically preempts anyone of the right of using the best and most effective means of providing health protection for the public. Further, it is interesting that the same bills single out tobacco as a product for which the Federal Trade Commission must recognize limitations in the exercise of its regulatory powers. An increasingly informed and concerned public is beginning to ask more questions about the privileged sanctuary and, apparently, untouchable status of tobacco.

Tobacco is, after all, a substance whose combustion byproducts are assimilated by the body. These products number in the hundreds, are pharmacologically active, and many are regarded as being harmful. Rarely is cigarette smoke described as beneficial to bodily function. Many other products with properties far less suspect have either been removed from the market or required to label in detail all possible undesirable effects and rigidly follow closely regulated advertising policies. It would seem, to date, that tobacco has been able to classify itself in a category that is unique and quite invulnerable to acceptable standards of governmental scrutiny and regulation.

Past experience has shown that had cigarettes been made of cranberries, for example, effective action would come with a far less strain.

Is it unreasonable to expect that an industry which manufactures a product, that does now, and will yet, adversely affect the lives of hundreds of thousands of people, state clearly on their packaging the possible undesirable effects caused by the use of their product? Is such an industry really free of all responsibility and liability for the harm they incur? Are they to be allowed the unlimited promotion of this product on public airways with advertising that is receiving an increasing amount of public censure?

For the above reasons, I urgently request you to support legislation which will: 1) cause that realistic statement of hazard, as well as the tar and nicotine content of each cigarette, be printed on each pack and be an integral part of all cigarette advertising; 2) progressively and effectively reduce the tar and nicotine yield per cigarette; 3) provide funds for effective health education in schools; and 4) remove from radio and television all cigarette advertising.

Cigarette Advertising Should Not Be Restricted

Fred S. Royster

When Fred S. Royster testified before the U.S. Congress in 1969, he was a tobacco grower working in the southeastern United States. In this extract from his testimony he argues against restricting cigarette advertising, stating that there is not enough medical proof that tobacco use is a health danger and that the government therefore should not impose regulations that hurt the tobacco industry. Royster also criticizes the surgeon general's report of 1964, which, he argues, highlights the hazards of smoking and ignores the benefits, aside from a cursory mention. Tobacco is an important cash crop for hundreds of thousands of Americans, brings in money through the tobacco tax, and has served as a symbol of relaxation and contentment throughout wars and conflicts, Royster points out.

In addition to the punitive taxation of tobacco and tobacco products, the smoking and health controversy continues. The anti-tobacco forces from within and out of the Government are stepping up their efforts to destroy our great industry. This is being done through propaganda and accusations regarding an alleged causal relationship between smoking and health. These accusations still lack the authority of medical proof based on the findings of scientific research. Almost all of the evidence presented thus far has been statistical allegations, which are the products of surveys and computer tapes.

The answer to most of our tobacco problems must be found through additional intensive research. There are far too many unknowns to justify the condemnation of our great to-

Fred S. Royster, testimony before the U.S. House of Representatives Committee on Interstate and Foreign Commerce, Washington DC, April 23, 1969.

bacco industry. We are indeed pleased that additional funds have been made available for accelerated tobacco research in certain areas.

Indeed, the tobacco community has everything to gain, and nothing to lose from research. If there is something in cigarettes that is harmful to humans, we want to find out what it is, and the sooner, the better, so it can be removed.

This is a complex and complicated problem. There are those, including myself, who believe the reason no one has established through medical research that cigarettes are responsible for human diseases is for the very good reason that they are not responsible.

Before saying more about the grower positions, I wish to make it clear that growers do not hold the view that consideration of their economic need is paramount to consideration of the health of people. The persons for whom I speak favor and encourage further and extensive medical and scientific research. We think that the truth should be sought and, if there is a tobacco causal relationship, it will be discovered.

The Government Should Be Fair

What we say, and with all the sincerity and force with which we are capable, is that the federal government in dealing with this acute and tremendous problem should deal with it at the very highest level of sovereign policy making. It should deal preemptively at the Congressional level. Further, the sovereign, through its Congress, should give a very careful, conservative and fair consideration to all of the persons whose fate may be determined by their action. We submit that the most fundamental foundation of a sound government is its dispensing of justice. I think that the most important thing which I will say today is to beseech that you, "The Congress", handle this matter and handle it with complete temperateness and fairness to the growers of tobacco as well as to all others.

I am not a doctor or a scientist or a statistician. Therefore, I have no expert opinion on the technical phases of the matters which are being presented to you. However, I have been informed that there is no satisfactory scientific proof of any causal connection between tobacco and disease. There is a complete difference of opinion on this subject among scientific men. Certainly there is not such proof as to justify a conviction of tobacco and an economic death sentence against the growers and manufacturers.

I also urge upon you that any final conclusion with respect to labeling and advertising should be reached only after there has been a careful and judicious balancing of the good of tobacco against any supposed or suspected danger of tobacco.

Benefits of Tobacco

I am sure that you have heard a great deal already, or will hear from others, more knowledgeable than I, about the economic benefits which our country has received from the tobacco business and the tobacco trade since colonial days—for example, the value of the exports, the assistance of tobacco in maintaining a balance of trade, the tremendous take by the government from the tobacco tax and from other taxes indirectly flowing from the growing and manufacture and sale of tobacco. I have said something about putting onto the scales the economic devastation which would come to growers if tobacco is sentenced and executed. To all of that I would like now to add something about the good accomplished by tobacco, other than economic benefits.

We people who grow tobacco and our predecessors for many generations have believed that we were in an honorable business. We have believed that in important respects tobacco is beneficial to the user.

There seems to be no doubt but that the use of tobacco in its various forms is relaxing, is enjoyable and is conducive to a measure of contentment.

In complete disagreement with those who attack tobacco most savagely as an evil thing, we growers believe that we have made a contribution to society by producing good tobacco.

Relationship with Stress

There is something about the stress and strain and stark reality of war which spotlights certain truths. In our wars of the last half century, nearly every soldier coming out of the battle reached for a cigarette. Nearly every sailor coming off watch went for a cigarette and a cup of coffee. When our soldiers were among foreign people, their most acceptable tokens of friendship were candy bars and cigarettes.

In World War I, in World War II, in the Korean War, the U.S.O. [United Service Organizations], the Red Cross, the Salvation Army, the tobacco companies, thousands of citizens, and the United States of America sent billions of cigarettes to our soldiers, to our allies and to our defeated foes. We believed that we were doing good. We still so believe.

The growers of tobacco were told that they were contributing to the war effort. We believed that we were so contributing. We still so believe.

Tensions and moments of extreme satisfaction and happiness seem to call for a smoke. The consumption of cigarettes always increases most rapidly in war periods.

Today is a day of tensions as never before in peace time. Who has tried to measure the relief from present day tensions which may be credited to tobacco? Who can predict what would be the explosion of tense people if there were no relaxing agents or avenues? We say that there is good in tobacco. It is much easier and much more exciting to denounce than to praise. We submit that there has been too much denouncing of tobacco and too little realistic balancing of the good of tobacco against possible but unproved hazards. I speak for to-bacco—in praise of tobacco.

For more than three centuries men and women have enjoyed the relaxation, the mental contentment and the pleasure that they have found in smoking.

The compilers of the Surgeon General's report agree with me. They say: "The significant beneficial effects of smoking occur primarily in the area of mental health, and the habit originates in a search for contentment."

The Committee then spent some 387 pages in measuring the alleged hazards and basically by statistics.

Individual Decision

The decision to smoke or not to smoke, the decision as to how much to smoke, are decisions for each individual adult. Each must and does balance the considerations for and against smoking—balance the relaxation, contentment, and enjoyment he gets against the expense, the ashes and any possible danger which may come from smoking. That is a decision which is constantly being made. It is a decision which people numbering more than half of our adult population have made in favor of smoking. There can be no more convincing proof that there is some good—indeed much good—in tobacco.

So, we submit that the adult individual in this country should and will continue to have and to exercise his own judgment and make his own decision as to whether to smoke and how much.

It seems that neither the Surgeon General's Committee nor the Surgeon General nor the Federal Trade Commission made any effort to measure the good of tobacco or to use it in the balancing in reaching their conclusion to condemn tobacco. For the growers of tobacco I submit to the policy-making Congress of our Government that careful and fair consideration should be given to that important element.

Warnings Are Unfair

The growers heartily concur in what the spokesmen for the cigarette industry and for advertising media have said against requiring caution notices to accompany all cigarette advertising. A vendor should not be required to disparage his wares. To require such, it seems to us, is cruel and unusual punishment and would be intemperate and vindictive action. We submit that it would be so construed not only by those who are punished (namely; the grower and manufacturer and the advertising media), but also by all smokers and by the general public. We fear that the tobacco industry, growers and manufacturers, could not long survive such punishment.

Notwithstanding any consideration of economics or the good of tobacco, the growers believe that the users of tobacco are entitled to information based on sound scientific studies and conclusions. But it seems to us that additional or stronger warnings are not needed. For the past several years it appears that the matter has been given about as much publicity as is possible to give a subject.

We have studied at length and fully discussed the numerous pieces of pending legislation under consideration here today by your committee. . . .

In conclusion, I wish to reiterate and make it abundantly clear that tobacco growers do not hold the view that consideration of their economic need is paramount to consideration of the health of people. We feel that there are far too many unknowns to arrive at the conclusion of placing further restrictions on our industry. Accelerated medical and scientific research is required to find the answers to this complex and complicated problem regarding smoking and health. Until these answers are found, I appeal to your wisdom, to your sense of fairness and justice. I rely on your common sense.

Fighting Nicotine Addiction

Sally Squires

Sally Squires has written about health and medical issues for the Washington Post *for almost three decades. In this article first published in the 1980s, Squires describes the growing antismoking movement of the time and the struggles of smokers to give up the habit. The health risks of smoking had finally been confirmed and generally accepted by the public, and many organizations were working to help people quit. The American Cancer Society began the Great American Smokeout day in 1977 to encourage all smokers to stop smoking for twenty-four hours. Squires also discusses the power of nicotine addiction and scientific research about withdrawal from the drug.*

This is it. Throw away the cigarettes. Bury the ashtrays. Take a long, deep breath. The Great American Smokeout—the best day of the year for smokers to quit—begins at midnight.

At no other time is there such widespread support for taking the courageous step of kicking the nicotine habit. Tomorrow, smokers will find encouragement not just from the American Cancer Society, sponsor of the annual event, but also from businesses, worksites and restaurants.

Some 5 million smokers went 24 hours without lighting up during last year's [1984] Smokeout. The idea is to experience being smoke-free for one day, "even if it's just to prove to themselves that they can do it," says a bulletin from the American Cancer Society.

If some smokers try it, like it and never light up again, well then, all the better. They can join the swelling ranks of former smokers—at last count some 35 million people have kicked the habit since 1964, the date of the landmark surgeon general's report linking cigarettes to cancer.

The Cost of Smoking

There's no need to elaborate on all the health benefits of quitting. The risk of lung cancer. Emphysema. The higher incidence of cancer of the esophagus, pancreas, bladder and kidney. The earlier onset of menopause for women and wrinkling of the skin. Smokers know all that.

Smokers also know better than anyone else the hassles and the mess of smoking: The deep, throaty hack, the stained teeth and the tobacco breath. The smell that lingers in clothes, carpeting and drapes, anything that absorbs the billows of smoke, not to mention the cigarette burns in carpet and furniture.

They also know the cost. Not just the $1.25 a pack, but the extra time lost from work. Smokers have more colds than nonsmokers, and their children have more inner ear infections than children who live in a smoke-free home. And there is growing evidence that the nonsmoking spouses of smokers have higher rates of heart and lung diseases.

Smokers are sometimes ridiculed for not having the gumption to give up cigarettes, or face a holier-than-thou attitude from people who have quit. "When [President] Ike Eisenhower quit smoking," says psychologist Jack Henningfield of the Addiction Research Center run by the National Institute on Drug Abuse, "he used to carry around a pack of cigarettes and offer them to people. When they took a cigarette, Eisenhower considered them a weak-willed SOB."

With the growing militancy among nonsmokers, Surgeon General C. Everett Koop recently predicted a limitation on where smokers will be allowed to light up. "The person that smokes in 1995 is going to have to smoke alone or with other smokers," Koop said. That might mean smoking in the bathroom, in the backyard or in a segregated area. "I wouldn't be surprised," he said, to see smoking limited to "out of doors."

Businesses are also jumping on the antismoking bandwagon, by restricting smoking to certain areas and sometimes banning it altogether from the worksite. One firm warned smokers that they would have to pay higher health care insurance premiums out of their own pockets if they didn't give up smoking. The company then gave smokers a year to quit, provided smoking cessation programs, and 12 months later charged a $300 fee to employees who still smoked.

More Knowledge About Nicotine

Today, with the benefit of growing research on nicotine, no one suggests that it is a snap to quit—nor do they consider kicking the habit an impossible task. The smoking field, says University of Michigan psychologist Ovide Pomerleau, "has come a long way from the time when we looked at smoking in a moralistic way."

Nicotine is a complex drug with a multitude of effects on the body, including the unique ability both to stimulate and to sedate. Research is producing new knowledge about effective ways to quit smoking—not for a few days or a few weeks, but for good. The goal is to achieve a smoke-free society by the year 2000.

Scientists are getting new insight into withdrawal. "We're merging psychology with pharmacology," Pomerleau says. Recent ex-smokers report feeling irritable, anxious and emotional. Some say they have trouble concentrating, experience slight memory changes and worsened muscle coordination. Headaches, nausea, sleep disturbances and gastrointestinal problems are also on the list of withdrawal symptoms.

How to Quit

But the good news is that these symptoms, when they occur, don't last for very long—at most a few days to two weeks. And thanks to the marriage of psychology and pharmacology, smokers now may get a doctor's prescription for a nicotine-

A Smoker's Musings

In this personal narrative Mike Sager, a writer for Esquire *magazine, describes his fears of stopping smoking.*

Afraid to stop smoking. This image I have: standing in a huge crowd, just another one of the assholes, another penitent, confused, judgmental, gullible follower, nodding my head, toeing the line, counting calories, counting grams of fat, counting heartbeats with a crook-wristed hand resting Jack Benny–like on the artery in my neck, climbing stairs and riding bikes that go nowhere, walking on a treadmill, for chrissakes (talk about your ugly metaphors), another smug, pitiful, politically correct nonsmoker squinting and grimacing and wrinkling my nose, dismissing the noxious fumes that I loved so well with a series of fey, intolerant little waves—just another hypocrite with a constant guilty craving for a cigarette.

Mike Sager, *"Smoking: A Love Story,"*
Esquire, *February 1998.*

containing chewing gum, called Nicorette, which may help ease withdrawal symptoms of some people who are severely addicted to cigarettes.

But the gum isn't the answer for everyone. People with gastrointestinal problems often find that the gum irritates their stomachs. Those with dentures usually can't chew it, and some people complain that to get the nicotine out of the gum, it is necessary to chew very hard.

Another approach is to wean smokers off nicotine by having them switch to lower-tar, lower-nicotine brands of cigarettes. But there's a catch: Many people "won't smoke these cigarettes" because they don't taste as good, Dr. Michael Russell, a smoking researcher from England, told the World Congress on Smoking Cessation recently. "And those that do smoke them tend to compensate" by smoking and inhaling more. Unless smokers continue to switch brands every week or so and consciously make an effort to inhale less, the nicotine and tar levels remain pretty much the same.

The claim is that most ex-smokers "just quit"—cold turkey and on their own—says the Addiction Research Center's Henningfield, who studies nicotine and other drugs. But interviews with many ex-smokers show, Henningfield says, that in fact they "actually go through a pretty elaborate routine" before kicking the habit. This includes gearing themselves psychologically for quitting, targeting a date to quit, and figuring out what to do instead of smoking.

The bottom line is hard work, willpower and a strong desire to succeed.

Questioning Nicotine Addiction

Ernest Van Den Haag

Social critic Ernest Van Den Haag writes extensively about issues concerning libertarianism, a school of thought that emphasizes free will. In this excerpt from a 1990 article he published in the National Review *magazine, Van Den Haag makes the unusual argument that most smokers are not addicted to nicotine. Instead, he writes, most people have "an ingrained habit" that they do not wish to stop and therefore blame it on addiction. Van Den Haag describes his own fondness for cigars to demonstrate his point: He enjoys the sheer act of smoking and is annoyed by the nicotine, which makes him jumpy, he writes. Van Den Haag concludes that most smokers should be able to quit if they resolve to do so.*

Opponents of smoking have a good case: smoking does increase health risks. Nonetheless, many people continue to smoke. According to non-smokers, they are addicted to nicotine. Is that so?

Many smokers have given up their habit. They managed to surmount the obvious difficulties more easily than people who try to give up overeating. The comparative case hardly suggests an addiction—unless by addiction we mean an ingrained habit and not an ineluctable physical craving, in which case "addiction" becomes a *façon de parler* [way of speaking].

If they are not addicted, why do the remaining smokers not stop, in view of the known health risks? Perhaps some do indeed continue because they have come to crave the effects of nicotine. They really have become addicted and suffer physi-

Ernest Van Den Haag, "The Smokescreen of Addiction," *National Review,* vol. 42, November 5, 1990, pp. 84–86. Copyright © 1990 by National Review, Inc., 215 Lexington Avenue, New York, NY, 10016. Reproduced by permission.

cal difficulties when they stop smoking. However, that is not the case of all smokers. I think it is the case of only a few. Probably most people smoke regardless of, and some even despite, nicotine. I smoke cigars, because I like smoking them. Actually the nicotine annoys me. It prevents me from smoking as many cigars as I would like: doing so would make me too jumpy because of the nicotine. I don't smoke in the evening because the nicotine interferes with my sleep. I would smoke more if someone invented cigars that taste as good as the ones I currently smoke, without the nicotine I'm presumed to crave.

How about alcohol? Like nicotine, alcohol has physiological effects. Many people drink for the sake of these effects, which they like. They want to be "relaxed" by alcohol, or to get drunk. However, I like the taste of wine, beer, liqueur. If someone invented a drink with the taste of these but without alcohol, I would drink far more than I do now. Alcohol does nothing for my mood other than making me tired. (I don't care to get drunk.)

Nobody knows how many smokers smoke despite and not because of nicotine, how many drinkers drink despite and not because of the inebriating effects of alcohol. Why assume that most smokers or drinkers want mainly nicotine or alcohol?

If it is not, at least not always, the nicotine or the alcohol, why do people smoke or drink? Why do babies suck their thumbs? Surely not for nicotine or alcohol. Since being weaned from their mothers' breasts, most people like to put something in their mouths. Some of us satisfy that longing by eating or drinking even when there is no physical need, or by smoking. Some just chew gum. One may exhort smokers to stop because of the health risk. But it is silly to label them addicted because they won't stop. After all, people habitually take many other health risks—in driving, or crossing the street, or eating the wrong foods—without being alleged to be "addicted."

Addiction Has Been Exaggerated

Addiction is an overextended concept. It appears now to describe any habit we disapprove of, perhaps because "addiction" enables us to disapprove of habits without blaming the person who develops them. A seductive idea: we can blame the dealer or manufacturer who makes a profit (horrors) while conveniently exonerating our friends. They suffer from a disease for which they cannot be blamed, although they volunteer. Not least, there are many juicy jobs for researchers and professionals who will treat, if not cure, addicts for the volitional weakness euphemistically depicted as a disease. They have a considerable stake in the thing.

Perhaps it is too hard for optimistic and rationalistic Americans to face the fact that many people who smoke or drink too much do what they want, even though it is bad for them. Some are self-destructive. Others indulge short-term satisfaction despite long-term risks. Still others are semi-addicted. [Austrian father of psychoanalysis] Sigmund Freud knew that his cigars aggravated his oral cancer. He gave them up for six months but couldn't write. So he resumed. Was it the nicotine? Would nicotine injections have satisfied him? Or was it the act of smoking and the taste of cigars? . . .

Real addicts who want to be helped should get all the psychological support—such as Alcoholics Anonymous—we can give. But there is no use pretending that every persistent smoker is a nicotine addict, even though it makes the non-smokers feel better to think so, or that everyone who likes to drink is an alcoholic. Nor is it sensible to believe that either is necessarily sick and cannot help himself. On the contrary, he cannot be helped by others unless he really wants to help himself. Their help consists of supporting his decision. He may not want to make that decision. Those who try to change the habits of the smoker or drinker who does not want to stop may themselves be "addicted" to telling others how to live and die.

P.S.: As we all know, Japanese live longer, on the average, than Americans, probably because the Japanese eat little meat, hardly any dairy foods, and lots of fish and rice. (Might one say Americans are addicted to meat and dairy food?) The Japanese also smoke more than Americans do. This does not show that smoking prolongs your life. It does demonstrate, however, that smoking shortens life less decisively than diet does.

Tobacco Litigation of the 1990s

Robert L. Rabin

Between 1995 and 1998 forty-six states sued the top tobacco companies in the country in order to seek compensation for costs of caring for smokers who developed health problems. The states argued that the tobacco industry had misled the public about the dangers of smoking. In 1998 the states and the tobacco companies agreed to the "Master Settlement," in which the tobacco companies would pay $206 billion to the states over twenty-five years. In the following excerpt from his book Regulating Tobacco, *Stanford University law professor Robert L. Rabin outlines the key points of the cases leading up to the settlement and the eventual terms of the deal. Rabin argues that the tobacco industry actually benefited in some ways from the settlement, which freed the tobacco companies from any further liability to the states. In addition, although the Master Settlement restricted the advertising and promotion of cigarettes to the youth, tobacco companies would not be penalized if the planned reductions in teen smoking were not met. Ironically, Rabin notes, after the settlement the states were using some of the tobacco company payments for projects that were unrelated to public health concerns.*

In June 1997 the states and the major tobacco companies reached a "global settlement," in reality, a detailed legislative proposal that was presented to Congress as an effort to virtually extinguish the tobacco wars. The tobacco industry, which for more than forty years had proudly proclaimed its invincibility from product liability, was now prepared to underwrite the largest civil settlement ever, paying $368.5 billion over 25 years to bring an end to the third wave of aggregate claims. In

Robert L. Rabin, *Regulating Tobacco.* New York: Oxford University Press, 2001. Copyright © 2001 by Oxford University Press. Reproduced by permission.

addition, the proposed legislative package would have bound the industry to an array of public health proposals, including acknowledgment of FDA [Food and Drug Administration] jurisdiction to engage in constrained regulation of nicotine; agreement to a "look back" provision under which the industry would be subject to fines linked to failure to reduce underage smoking according to targeted goal and timelines; and bans on billboard advertising, use of human and cartoon figures in ads, and brand-name sponsorship of sporting events and promotional merchandise.

The Tobacco Industry Sought Protection from Further Lawsuits

Beyond doubt, the June 1997 agreement is a testament to the awesome threat posed by the litigation strategy. What the industry was willing to buy, at a considerable price, was relief from litigation uncertainty. This latter point is underscored by the concessions offered by the antitobacco forces in the proposal; in other words, the industry's quid pro quo [equal exchange]. Under the plan, the state health care reimbursement suits would have been settled and the industry would have been granted immunity from all other forms of class action. Thus, in one fell swoop, the industry would have eliminated its greatest nightmare—the prospect of catastrophic loss from a cluster of state recoupments, certified classes of tort[1] claimants, or third-party sources such as Blue Cross or union health plans, successfully convincing juries that the industry's past course of conduct warranted potential multibillion-dollar recoveries in compensatory and punitive damages for the legions of injury victims represented in the particular cases. Moreover, under still another provision in the settlement plan, there would have been no punitive damages allowed in individual cases for industry conduct prior to the enactment by Congress of the legislation. Once again, this provision directly

---

1. A tort is damage for which a civil suit can be brought.

targeted a massive source of uncertainty—the prospect of a breakthrough in individual cases with one jury after another reacting with vehemence against the narrative of industry deceit. A third provision would have capped the total annual liability for awards on future individual claims at $5 billion, a considerable sum, but nonetheless a fixed cap that would contribute from yet another perspective to the predictability that the industry sought.

There were other restrictions on litigation as well, but the point is clear. The state health care cases may have rested on dubious theoretical premises. But a realistic assessment of the threat presented by potential catastrophic loss litigation requires more than just finely honed theoretical analysis. By mid-1997, the industry faced the prospect of being sued by virtually every state in the country, represented on a retainer basis by a cadre of the most experienced and skilled tobacco lawyers, pressing a variety of common law and statutory claims. Other third-party claims lurked in the background. The documents told a tale of industry deceit and indifference to public health considerations. Could trial court judges in every, or virtually all, state health care recovery cases be counted on to enter summary judgment,[2] or would the industry be at the mercy of juries exposed to the tale of industry wrongdoing? . . .

Harsher Legislation Is Proposed

What the negotiating parties failed to recognize was that once their "settlement" reached the halls of Congress, it would take on a life of its own. Almost immediately, as the wave of anti-industry public sentiment crested, a far more draconian legislative proposal emerged. The McCain bill would have obligated the industry to pay $516 billion over 25 years, and, even more strikingly, the bill incorporated virtually all of the earlier

---

2. A summary judgment is a judgment offered by the court prior to a verdict because no body of facts exists and the parties are entitled to a judgment by law.

negotiated public health provisions while eliminating the industry's hard-fought quid pro quo—the litigation immunity provisions. Perhaps inevitably, a reversal of the legislative tide occurred, bolstered by an urgent industry advertising blitz and the backing of industry congressional supporters. And, in the end, no federal legislation was enacted.

As the congressional battle waxed and waned, the industry—perhaps as a strategy to promote a new image in timely fashion—settled individually with the four states that were closest to trial and that, with one exception (Texas), probably presented the greatest threat of a litigation setback: Mississippi, Florida, Texas, and Minnesota. In the absence of these settlements, one might well have concluded, as the congressional deliberations collapsed in June 1998, that the third-wave aggregation strategy had yielded precious little beyond massive additional documentation of industry wrongdoing.

But the four individual state settlements did amount to some $40 billion, to be paid out over 25 years. And within a year, in November 1998, the industry and the 46 remaining states had negotiated a $206 billion settlement of all outstanding state health care reimbursement claims, considerably less in industry payout than the failed June 1997 agreement, but, on the other hand, the agreement contained none of the immunity provisions from class action litigation and punitive damages included in that earlier package.

The Master Settlement

In the end, it is hard to assess the significance, if any, of the health care reimbursement litigation. The so-called Master Settlement, which extinguished any further liability of the industry to the states, contained a scaled-back version of the public health provisions in the earlier 1997 agreement, with some remaining restrictions on advertising and promotion aimed at the youth market: billboard advertising was banned and brand name sponsorship of recreational activities was limited, among other things. But no longer were there any provisions for industry "look back" penalties if scheduled reductions in teenage smoking were not met. No longer was there any mention of acknowledging FDA jurisdiction—a separate battleground then before the Supreme Court, which subsequently ruled against the FDA, on the agency's independent assertion of regulatory authority. No longer was there certainty that the costs of smoking would rise appreciably; estimates were that, as a result of the settlement, the price of a pack of cigarettes would rise a relatively modest 35 cents over five years, and the agreement contained set-off provisions for federal tax increases and product sales downturns that served as potential further qualifiers. Indeed, no longer was there any assurance that the states would spend a significant proportion of the industry payments on smoking reduction programs. To the contrary by early 2000 it was clear that the states were earmarking the funds for a variety of projects unrelated to tobacco control and, in many instances, bearing no relationship to public health concerns. Many argued, with some justification, that the major beneficiaries of the Master Settlement were the plaintiffs' lawyers, who stood to realize billions in attorneys' fees.

International Aspects of U.S. Government Tobacco Bills

Judith Mackay

Judith Mackay is a physician who works in the United Kingdom and has written extensively about global tobacco issues. In the following article Mackay outlines the impact of U.S. tobacco legislation on the rest of the world, especially on developing nations. She points out the majority of sales by U.S. tobacco companies are made overseas, mainly in developing countries. In 1997, as forty states were engaged in litigation against the tobacco industry, Senator John McCain introduced legislation to increase the money tobacco companies would have to pay the states from approximately $369 billion to $516 billion. McCain's legislation also provided for restrictions in marketing tobacco products to developing nations, Mackay writes. The McCain bill was defeated in June 1998. However, the U.S. State Department urged all of its embassy officials to stop acting on behalf of tobacco companies—thus exerting some measure of control on tobacco sales by American companies overseas.

When [C.E.] Koop et al published "Reinventing American Tobacco Policy" in [the *Journal of the American Medical Association,*] February 1998, they were hopeful that the US public health sector, legislators, and the community at large would finally grasp the political nettle of tobacco control, reining in the tobacco industry domestically and internationally. Their hope was misplaced; the tobacco settlement talks collapsed[1] and the US Senate voted to defeat a major tobacco

---

1. At various points in the 1990s, settlement money was awarded and repealed. Eventually, money was paid to most states that had filed lawsuits.

Judith Mackay, "International Aspects of US Government Tobacco Bills," *Journal of the American Medical Association,* vol. 28, no. 19, May 19, 1999, pp. 1,849–50. Copyright © 1999 by the American Medical Association. All rights reserved. Reproduced by permission.

control bill [the McCain tobacco bill] in June 1998.

Koop et al clearly described the tobacco industry's unwillingness to abide by ethical business rules and social standards, its ruthless marketing of an addictive lethal product, its denial of the health evidence, and its obstruction of government action to prevent and reduce the epidemic. These tactics are now universal. People throughout the world have been exposed to sophisticated and seductive tobacco promotional advertising, especially since the introduction of transglobal satellites, cable and Internet advertising, and paid product placement of cigarettes in motion picture films, as well as political obstruction to tobacco control action.

As cigarette markets shrink in the West, the tobacco companies seem determined to expand into the huge populations of the developing world. These US-based companies currently supply about 20% of the nearly 6 trillion cigarettes smoked in the world each year. As local, state, and federal antitobacco laws have reduced smoking by almost 20% during the past decade in the United States, tobacco companies have increased their exports by 260%. In 1996, for example, the top 2 US cigarette makers, Philip Morris and R. J. Reynolds Tobacco Co, sold, respectively, 70% and 57% of their products overseas.

By 2025, only 15% of the world's smokers will live in developed countries, and it is developing countries that will bear the brunt of the tobacco epidemic in the [twenty-first] century. By 2030, the World Health Organization predicts 10 million people will die annually from tobacco-related diseases, 70% in the developing world.

What Was the Settlement and What Difference Would It Have Made?

The 1997 US $368.5 billion settlement talks between 40 state attorney generals and the tobacco industry would have settled lawsuits by both smokers and states reclaiming tobacco-attributable health care costs. The settlement also would have restricted tobacco advertising and required producers to pay fines if smoking rates among youth did not decline. In return, the industry would have received protection from most types of lawsuits.[2]

In June 1997, tobacco control advocates from 19 countries supported the international components of the proposed settlement in a joint statement: "It is unacceptable to discuss a comprehensive settlement of the US tobacco litigation which does not include measures to control the use of US tobacco products outside of the United States." Signatories included representatives from Australia, Hong Kong, India, Japan, Malaysia, Mongolia, New Zealand, the Philippines, Taiwan, and Thailand.

Senator John McCain (R, Ariz) then introduced the McCain bill, which would have increased the settlement to US $516 billion and would have removed the legal protection sought by the industry. At this point, the industry withdrew from the settlement talks and tried to derail the McCain bill with an aggressive US $40 million advertising and political lobbying campaign.

The McCain bill also included international provisions that would have ended the use of US government funds to promote tobacco sales overseas, imposed strong antismuggling measures, called for a code of conduct mandating US-based companies to adhere to the same marketing and labeling standards overseas as they adhere to domestically, and created a US nongovernmental organization to fund international anti-tobacco organizations. These strong international provisions were progressively weakened in negotiations with the White House and others. Soon, the only meaningful international provision remaining was a commitment of $350 million an-

---

2. In the 1998 Master Settlement agreement, the tobacco industry was ordered to pay $206 billion to forty-six states over a twenty-five-year period.

nually to tobacco control worldwide. Even this was lost when the bill was defeated in June 1998.

The Influence of the Doggett Amendment

In the midst of all this, partly from a review of US tobacco policies overseas and partly from a legislative amendment championed by Rep Lloyd Doggett (D, Tex), the US State Department issued a cable to all of its embassies urging embassy officials to stop acting or lobbying on behalf of the tobacco industry, unless there are laws or regulations that they treat domestic and foreign tobacco products differently.

The Doggett amendment requires the US trade representative to consult with the US Department of Health and Human Services on all tobacco-related matters and to report to Congress within 10 days of taking up a tobacco-related issue. It prevents US governmental agencies from opposing tax increases; calls for bans on advertising, promotion, and sponsorship; requires stronger warning labels and ingredient disclosure laws; and allows the United States to intervene only if tobacco control measures are not applied to foreign and domestic products alike.

The Doggett amendment should prevent embassy officials from providing behind-the-scenes advice to tobacco companies to help them oppose tobacco control measures. It should also prevent US government officials from helping US tobacco companies promote their products by prohibiting them from such activities as speaking at tobacco company events or by prohibiting tobacco companies from sponsoring embassy events.

This news is especially welcome in Asia, where Japan, Taiwan, the Republic of Korea, and Thailand were threatened with trade sanctions unless they opened their markets and allowed advertising of US tobacco products. This threat resulted in a 10% increase in tobacco consumption in these countries over and above any expected increase. In February 1999, the

US State Department reissued the directive associated with the Doggett amendment in an effort to increase awareness among posts abroad. . . .

One global benefit of the recent litigation is that thousands of previously hidden tobacco industry documents have been made public, and many have been placed on the Internet. On July 17, 1998, President Clinton directed the Secretary of Health and Human Services to coordinate a review of these documents and develop a plan to make the documents more accessible to researchers and the public at large. These documents contain a wealth of inside information on tobacco advertising, the addictive nature of nicotine, the health consequences of tobacco use, and the effects of certain tobacco product designs and ingredients.

THE HISTORY OF DRUGS

CHAPTER 4

Current Issues and Controversies

Smoking Is More Dangerous than Previously Realized

Michele Late

Michele Late is executive editor of the Nation's Health, *which explores many topics relating to the well-being of American society. In the following viewpoint Late outlines the latest findings of the U.S. surgeon general, released on the fortieth anniversary of the 1964 surgeon general's first report on smoking. Scientists and doctors have discovered that not only does smoking cause lung cancer and emphysema, it also causes disease in almost every other part of the body—any part reached by the bloodstream. Late also describes the introduction of recent legislation to increase the regulation of tobacco companies, including a bill that would give the Food and Drug Administration the authority to regulate tobacco products.*

While smoking has long been linked to an array of health problems, recent research shows that the harmful habit is worse than previously known: A new report from the U.S. surgeon general found that smoking causes diseases in almost every organ of the human body.

Released in late May [2004], "The Health Consequences of Smoking: A Report of the Surgeon General," cites more than 1,600 scientific articles on the health effects of smoking. In addition to the well-known effects of smoking, such as lung, mouth and esophageal cancers, the new report found that smoking is conclusively linked to leukemia, cataracts and pneumonia as well as cancers of the pancreas, cervix and kidneys. Other complications linked to smoking in the report included diabetes complications, hip fractures and reproductive complications.

"The toxins from cigarette smoke can go everywhere the blood flows," said U.S. Surgeon General Richard Carmona, MD, MPH, FACS. "I'm hoping this new information will help motivate people to quit smoking and convince young people not to start in the first place."

The new report was released on the anniversary of the historic 1964 surgeon general's report on smoking, which was the first to draw widespread attention to the dangers of tobacco use. While U.S. smoking rates have notably dropped since the publication of the first report—42 percent of the public smoked in 1964 versus 22.5 percent of adults today—the practice still leads to 440,000 U.S. deaths each year.

More than 12 million Americans have died from smoking since the 1964 report, and another 25 million Americans alive today are expected to die of a smoking-related illness, according to the U.S. Department of Health and Human Services.

Among the report's other conclusions was that low-tar or low-nicotine cigarettes are not healthier than regular cigarettes.

Despite the damaging effects of tobacco use, quitting smoking has immediate and long-term effects such as improved circulation and a drop in heart rate, the report found. Even quitting late in life can have positive effects: Giving up tobacco at age 65 can reduce a smoker's risk of dying of related disease by 50 percent.

Legislation Introduced

The surgeon general report findings came as courts, legislators and advocates stepped up their attention to tobacco control in [2004].

In Washington, D.C., legislators from both sides of the political table embraced new legislation that would give the U.S. Food and Drug Administration [FDA] the authority to regulate tobacco products. . . .

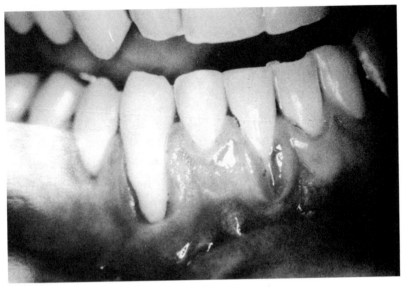

Smokeless tobacco caused extensive damage to this user's teeth and gums. National Cancer Institute

The bills would provide FDA with the authority for actions such as prohibiting unsubstantiated health claims, requiring changes in the composition of tobacco products to make them less harmful and protecting children from tobacco marketing. "A June [2004] poll by the Campaign for Tobacco-Free Kids [a public health advocacy group] found that 69 percent of respondents favored passing legislation that would provide regulation authority to FDA.

"Many consumers, including smokers, are surprised to learn that no federal agency has the authority to require tobacco companies to list the ingredients that are in their products—things like trace amounts of arsenic, formaldehyde and ammonia," [U.S. senator Mike] DeWine said. "No federal agency has the authority to inspect tobacco manufacturers—how the cigarette and smokeless tobacco products are made, whether the manufacturers' machines and equipment are clean."

FDA regulation of tobacco is supported by health and tobacco control advocates, including APHA [the American Public Health Association], which has long had policy on the books specifically calling for such a move. APHA also supports measures that would provide incentives to tobacco farmers to switch to other crops, such as a tobacco industry-financed buyout of such farmers.

Continuing the Fight

However, APHA and other tobacco control advocates were opposed to a taxpayer-financed buyout plan that was making its way through Congress in June [2004]. The measure, introduced in the House by Rep. Ron Lewis, R-Ky., would provide $9.6 billion over several years to tobacco growers to help them transition to new crops.

Unfortunately, the bill would do nothing to protect public health and would instead eliminate price and production controls, allowing tobacco to be grown anywhere, according to critics. Because the buyout would be funded by the existing federal cigarette tax, money could be diverted from the federal Children's Health Insurance Program, which is funded by the same tax.

The buyout would also provide most of its payments to large corporations, with 80 percent of recipients receiving only about $5,000 or less over five years, according to Environmental Working Group.

Such a plan would provide an "unwarranted windfall" to tobacco companies, said Matthew Myers, president of the Campaign for Tobacco-Free Kids.

"Tobacco companies benefit because they do not have to pay for the buyout and they end up with cheaper tobacco," Myers said. "The Congressional Research Service has estimated that tobacco companies will save between half a billion and $2 billion a year under such a buyout proposal. In contrast, tobacco farmers are left with no economic safety net and at the mercy of tobacco companies."

In late June [2004], measure had passed the House as part of H.R. 4520, a corporate tax bill, and tobacco control advocates were calling on senators to reject the language. APHA members contacted their senators in opposition to the buyout plan as part of an APHA action alert. The Association was also part of a letter sent in June to senators and representatives asking for their opposition.[1]

In the courts, a district judge ruled in May that the federal government can continue with its racketeering lawsuit against the tobacco industry. In the case, which began in 1999 and has been held up by challenges from tobacco companies, the U.S. Justice Department is working to hold the tobacco industry responsible for deceptive marketing and concealment of health risks.[2]

1. The bill was passed into law in October 2004.
2. As of December 2005, the U.S. government had concluded its presentation of the case and was awaiting the judge's decision.

A Baseball Player's Addiction to Smokeless Tobacco

Stan Grossfeld

Stan Grossfeld is an award-winning photojournalist and sports-writer for the the Boston Globe. *In this article he profiles Red Sox pitcher Curt Schilling and his long battle with dipping snuff—a form of smokeless tobacco known to cause oral cancer and long popular with baseball players. In 1998 the pitcher was diagnosed with a precancerous mouth lesion and told he must stop or almost certainly develop cancer, Grossfeld writes. However, Schilling has been unable to quit dipping, even after watching his own wife survive cancer and meeting another ballplayer dying of oral cancer. Schilling has tried to break his habit many times, once stopping for a year and a half before going back to dipping. Grossfeld notes that the U.S. Smokeless Tobacco Company refuses to discuss any claims of the health risks of using smokeless tobacco.*

For Red Sox pitcher Curt Schilling it is harder than firing a split-fingered fastball past [Yankee third baseman] Alex Rodriguez. Harder than beating the Yankees.

"It's obviously the hardest thing I've ever tried to do. Quit," said Schilling about his greatest opponent, smokeless tobacco. "And I still haven't done it yet."

It is an uncomfortable subject.

Schilling has battled the demons of smokeless or spit tobacco since he was 15, when a high school classmate dared him to try it. He liked it and was hooked.

Smokeless tobacco contains 28 cancer-causing agents, according to the National Cancer Institute. It has been linked to oral cancer, tooth and gum decay, and possibly heart disease,

.ccording to the American Cancer Society. The Surgeon General has testified before Congress that "smokeless tobacco does cause cancer." It also contains highly addictive nicotine.

In March 1998, Joe Garagiola, the former major league catcher and current chairman of Oral Health America's National Spit Tobacco Education Program (NSTEP), brought an oral health team to the spring training site of the Phillies, for whom Schilling was plying his trade at the time.

"Schilling was in a line to get checked," said Garagiola. "I could see that he was getting very edgy because he was thinking about the exam. I practically held him by the hand making sure he wouldn't leave. We were talking umpires and Yogi [Berra] stories, anything I could to keep him there. He comes out and he's as white as a sheet. He said the second they looked in his mouth the dentist said, 'If you were my son, I'd have this biopsied yesterday.'"

The results showed that Schilling had a lesion on his lower lip, a sign of abnormal cell changes, and a precursor to oral cancer.

Days later, a somber Schilling appeared at a press conference in Clearwater, Fla.

"It's bad," he began. "Basically in no uncertain terms they told me that if I were to continue I would have cancer. They were 100 percent sure of it. You wonder how the tobacco companies—the people that do this—can go to sleep at night. It's a drug, there's no doubt about it. It's addictive."

Stops and Starts

There are two types of spit tobacco sold in the United States. There's chewing tobacco, the leafy kind that comes in pouches; a "chaw" of tobacco gives you the puffed-out-cheek look of [Major League outfielder] Lenny Dykstra. Then there's moist snuff, sold in round cans, which comes cured, finely ground, and sometimes flavored. A pinch placed between the cheek and gum is called dipping. One pinch packs as much nicotine as nearly four cigarettes.

Schilling, who has used the moist snuff, went through two cans of Copenhagen a day for years. His father, a smoker, got cancer before he died in 1998 of a brain aneurysm. His wife is a skin cancer survivor. He told Garagiola he was worried for his kid.

"Schilling had the courage to talk about it publicly," said Garagiola.

In 1998, Schilling told *Time* magazine, "It got to where my gums were bleeding and my lower lip was like raw meat. I would stop for a day or two and then dip again."

He has tried to stop at least a dozen times. Once he tried to stop cold turkey for two weeks and became violently ill.

He stopped for a year and a half.

"I saw him at the All-Star Game at Fenway Park in 1999," said Garagiola. "He walks up to me and says to one of his kids, 'Gehrig, here's the man that saved Daddy's life.' I said, 'No, you saved your Daddy's life because he loves you so much.'"

Garagiola says he can recognize two things a mile away: A bad toupee and whether someone is dipping. When Garagiola ran into Schilling again in 2000 things were different. "He said, 'I was playing golf and one of the guys said, 'Aw, come on, one dip isn't going to hurt you and I was off and running.' I said 'OK, usually you fall off the horse seven times. This is your first time. Now get back on that horse.'"

When John Greene, the dentist who conducted the initial oral exam, returned to the Phillies spring training camp in 2000 for a checkup, Schilling was absent.

"I called him at home and he said, 'Doc, I'm embarrassed.' I told him if you can stop for a year, you can stop. I don't want to be critical of him. I give him a lot of credit, he keeps trying. Just criticize the product and the addiction," said

Greene, dean emeritus at the University of California–San Francisco's school of dentistry.

Greene said he watched on television as co-MVP [Most Valuable Player] Schilling was celebrating the 2001 World Series victory against the Yankees and saw that Schilling was still dipping. Asked if Schilling will get oral cancer, Greene said, "I think he will if he continues."

Schilling, a five-time All-Star, is known for his community service. He and his wife, Shonda, a melanoma survivor, have launched SHADE, The Curt and Shonda Schilling Melanoma Foundation of America, and have also raised more than $4 million to battle amyotrophic lateral sclerosis (Lou Gehrig's disease). But in a recent clubhouse interview when the subject of his own struggle against spit tobacco is broached, Schilling politely says he would rather not talk. Ironically, it was "World No Tobacco Day."

"I'm not really interested in talking about it because I'm still battling it," said Schilling. "It's not something I want to talk about. There's nothing to talk about. I haven't quit."

Nearly half of the current Red Sox use spit tobacco, higher than the 36 percent average in Major League Baseball, according to a 2003 study by the Oregon Research Institute.

Recipe for Cancer

The American Cancer Society estimates that 27,260 new cases of oral cancer will be detected [in 2004], resulting in 7,230 deaths.

Among the ingredients in spit tobacco are cancer-causing substances such as nitrosamines and benzopyrene as well as toxic materials such as cadmium (found in car batteries), polonium 210 (in nuclear waste), uranium 235 (in nuclear weapons), and formaldehyde (in embalming fluid), according to Dr. Peggy Walsh, a professor at the University of San Francisco and a NSTEP consultant.

"Pair highly addictive nicotine with cancer-causing chemicals . . . that's a recipe for disaster," said Walsh.

Mike Bazinet, spokesman for U.S. Smokeless Tobacco Company, would not discuss the components of the company's tobaccos. "We don't make any health claims," he said. "We don't debate health issues in the media."

U.S. Smokeless expects record sales in 2004. It is the only part of the U.S. tobacco industry still growing. [In June 2004], legislation was introduced that would give the Food and Drug Administration [FDA] new powers to regulate smokeless tobacco.

U.S. Smokeless is trying to convince the FDA that its products are a safer alternative for the nearly 50 million adults who smoke in the U.S. They claim "tobacco harm reduction" is an alternative to the prevalent "quit or die" philosophy. One study from the University of Alabama claims the mortality rate of smokeless tobacco is only 2 percent that of cigarettes.

Dr. Greg Connolly, a scientific advisor for the Massachusetts Tobacco Control Program, says that research is funded by U.S. Smokeless and, "in my opinion, is biased by unrestricted grants."

"I hate statistics," said Garagiola. "Maybe because I never wanted to see my batting average flashed on the scoreboard. Hell no, it's not a safer alternative. What they're telling you is don't jump out of the 50th floor, jump out of the 30th floor. You're going to get killed either way."

Connolly acknowledges that spit tobacco is not as great a health risk as cigarettes, which have hundreds of carcinogens in them. But spit tobacco can still be lethal. "It's like shooting yourself in the foot instead of the head," he said.

[In 2003], U.S. Smokeless spent $72.5 million on advertising. Connolly says the company is targeting young adults with starter flavored tobaccos where the user "graduates" to more addictive nicotine products. "It's a gateway to cigarette smok-

use spit tobacco you are three times more likely to Connolly.

A Baseball Tradition

Connolly fears a return to the 1980s when Hall of Famers Carlton Fisk and George Brett were endorsing Skoal Bandits and one in five high school athletes in Massachusetts was using spit tobacco. The Centers for Disease Control recommends Nicorette gum, the nicotine patch, and cessation counseling instead of smokeless tobacco.

In the Red Sox clubhouse, Schilling says he has used the nicotine patch, herbal blends of snuff, and underwent counseling. "I've tried everything," he said.

Does being around ballplayers during the season make it harder to quit? Schilling shakes his head. "No, that would be making an excuse," he said. Asked why he uses, Schilling shrugs. "I don't know why, I really don't. I've quit for over a year and started back again so I can't put my finger on any one thing. I don't chew when I play or when I pitch."

Schilling has said that dipping dehydrates him so he doesn't do it while he's pitching or working out. He dips more in the offseason when he has time on his hands.

According to Garagiola, Schilling met Bill Tuttle, a former major leaguer who lost part of his jaw and cheek after getting oral cancer. Tuttle toured some MLB clubhouses before his death in 1998 and Oral Health America published a before-and-after poster of the former outfielder. In the first picture he's in his Minnesota Twins uniform with a big chunk of tobacco bulging in his cheek. That picture is titled, "Glory Days." Next to it is a picture of a disfigured Tuttle dying, his face swollen, his eyes shut. That photo is entitled, "Gory Days."

The image of Tuttle, who was 69 when he died, pains Schilling. "Oh, sure it does, sure it does. It's a weakness, you gotta be set and make a commitment to quit."

The Smoking Vaccine

Eddie Dean

In this selection from Men's Health *magazine, writer Eddie Dean discusses the promise of a smoking vaccine from a personal point of view. A longtime smoker who watched his own mother, also a smoker, die of throat cancer, Dean writes that he is desperate to stop smoking and is seeking a "miracle cure." He describes his visit to the lab of Nabi Biopharmaceuticals, one of the companies working to develop a vaccine, where he learns that the drug will work by preventing nicotine from entering the brain and delivering the high to which smokers are addicted. Nabi, a U.S. company, is competing with a British drug firm to create the first smoking vaccine to gain the approval of the U.S. Food and Drug Administration, Dean points out. However, it will be several years before a smoking vaccine is available to the public.*

Recently an old friend and mentor—a decorous southerner 15 years my senior—grabbed a cigarette from my pack of Camel Lights and tore off the end. "Smoking with a filter," he announced gravely, "is like using a condom." Then he fired up the shaggy blunt and exhaled a thick cloud of smoke. A former chain smoker, he hadn't taken so much as a puff in the months since the last time we'd met.

The lucky bastard.

He's one of the few who have learned to flirt with the foul weed only when the whim moves them. As for the rest of us, the more than 25 million male smokers in the United States, we curse [sixteenth-century British smoking advocate] Sir Walter Raleigh, as John Lennon once put it, and reach for another cigarette. . . .

My family gives me three good reasons to want to quit, and that desire, experts say, is crucial to having a fighting

Eddie Dean and Erin Hobday, "The Smoking Vaccine," Men's Health, vol. 19, December 2004, pp. 176–82. Copyright © 2004 by Rodale, Inc. Reproduced by permission.

chance. Even so, I have to admit that a prime motivator is fear: Watching your mother die of cancer can do that to you.

All I need now is a miracle cure, a shot of medicine to take away the kick that keeps me hooked on nicotine. This isn't as far-fetched as it may seem. Two companies are vying to develop a vaccine that would neutralize nicotine's hold on the brain by keeping it from getting there in the first place. In theory, this would turn smoking into a buzzless bore. If either of them succeeds, millions of men like me could trash their soft packs for good, reducing our risk of dozens of ailments, including heart disease, stroke, and 10 different types of cancer.

Beginning the Vaccine Investigation

The science behind the vaccines is as cut-and-dried as a tobacco leaf hanging in a North Carolina barn. Both vaccines are designed to stimulate antibodies in the bloodstream that recognize and bond with nicotine, and prevent it from entering the brain. Stop nicotine from crossing the blood-brain barrier and it can't perform its chemical seduction on our hapless neurons. Thus, the mighty cigarette, or what the big tobacco firms like to refer to as a "delivery system," delivers everything except the high. And that's no way to satisfying your jones.

It sounds too good to be true, especially for a skeptical, chain-smoking reporter. So I make the two-cigarette drive from my home to the research and development offices of Nabi Biopharmaceuticals in Rockville, Maryland. The company touts its vaccine, NicVax, as a revolutionary approach to tobacco-addiction treatment. "It's based on the assumption that the main reason smokers can't quit is that they miss the rush they get when the nicotine hits the brain" says Henrik Rasmussen, M.D., Ph.D., of Nabi. "We are basically attempting to block that, so you lose the feeling of well-being that cigarettes give you."...

He mentions that a competitor, Pfizer, is developing its own antismoking drug that also blocks the nicotine receptors in the brain. "The problem is that it's a tablet you take once a day. If you're a passionate smoker and you're missing your rush, you stop taking your pill. Then, 3 days later, you puff a cigarette and you're back in trouble."

Nabi is betting the NicVax vaccine offers a lot more protection than that. Eight shots at a doctor's office over a 12-month period will cover patients for the year, which researchers have found is a critical time period to prevent smokers from lighting up again. "With NicVax, you're stuck," says Dr. Rasmussen. "And that's what you need. Studies have shown that if you make it past a year without relapse, your chances of staying smoke-free are very good."

This all struck me as fine for him to say, in his tidy scientist's office ... but it still seemed too pat, too rational, and far too optimistic. Smokers are a tough, stubborn, often gloomy, generally hopeless lot, and a laboratory rat never has to face the temptation of a cig offered along with a pint of beer at a bar.

If I left the Nabi offices unconvinced, my doubts diminished somewhat when I discovered that the government is putting its money on NicVax—the National Institute on Drug Abuse (NIDA) has given Nabi a healthy dose of funding to carry out clinical trials at the University of Minnesota, the University of Nebraska, and the University of Wisconsin. "This is a new paradigm, and it's working on the concept of drug priming," says Francis Rocci, Ph.D., a researcher on nicotine addiction at the NIDA. "If someone had a relapse and picked up a cigarette, he wouldn't get the priming effect of smoking. The vaccine blocks the nicotine spike that can take you from two cigarettes at a party Friday night to running down to the 7-Eleven and buying a pack on Saturday morning."

Rocci says NicVax may have an added benefit, since nicotine molecules that are blocked from reaching the brain dissolve in the bloodstream. "This could be therapeutic, somewhat like a patch" he says. "It releases the nicotine into the blood at a very slow rate, so you won't get a buzz, but it will probably keep smokers from going into withdrawal."

Of course, as with every so-called smoking cure, the proof is in the puffing, or the lack thereof. Based on the just-released results of the NIDA-funded phase 2 trials mentioned previously, NicVax looks like a pretty effective buzz kill: Thirty-three percent of the smokers receiving the highest dose of NicVax quit smoking for a month or more. (And even the folks who didn't stay smoke-free on NicVax lit up a lot less.) "I went from 30 cigarettes a day, down to 10, and then for some reason I hung on to two a day for an awfully long time," says Phil, a 56-year-old construction foreman who joined the trial to beat a 4-decade smoking habit. "It was like, okay, I'm not getting anything from smoking, so why am I doing it? By the end of the study, I had quit."

Killing the Craving

In the race to save our lungs and our lives, Nabi faces serious competition from Xenova, a British drug firm that's developing a similar vaccine, Ta-Nic. Xenova has recently completed phase 1 clinical trials, and after 6 weeks, nearly half of the participants voluntarily gave up smoking or reported reduced pleasure when smoking. Xenova CEO David Oxlade is cautiously optimistic about his vaccine, which he says won't be available for several years. He also provides an important caveat: "This vaccine will take away the high," he says, "but it won't take away the craving."

Ah, the craving. That's what smokers like me dread the most. Beyond the physical addiction is the phantom limb of the lost plume of smoke, forever just out of reach. Yet, even with this aspect of withdrawal, the vaccines may be helpful, albeit in an indirect way. When I questioned former smokers, they all told me that the longer you can stay off the cigs, the less craving you'll have. So if Ta-Nic (and NicVax, for that matter) can help people string together a significant stretch of smokeless days, the urge to light up should eventually lose its power.

"The majority of people who have quit at 3 months on treatments such as Zyban are smoking again within a year," Oxlade says. "They can't stay abstinent for more than a year, and that's where the vaccine is really breaking new ground. It does much more than take away the high and the pleasure; it stops the readdiction cycle. The goal here is to allow people to remain abstinent."

Asking an Addict

Oxlade is another ex-smoker who quit without a magic bullet like Ta-Nic. But I need the voice of a fellow traveler, an expert who knows firsthand the pull of a Pall Mall [cigarette] and can cast a somewhat colder eye on these vaccines. I speak by phone with Kathleen Kantak, Ph.D., a professor of psychology at Boston University, who has done extensive research on cocaine and tobacco addiction. As I chain-smoke my Camels, she's busy chewing a wad of nicotine gum. Though she hasn't smoked in years, she still needs her daily fix, even after weaning herself off the patch. Clearly, here is a scientist who respects the power of the object of her scrutiny, and she is wary of miracles, even the sort of double-blind-tested cures that drip from the end of a needle.

"On a theoretical level, these vaccines should work," says Kantak. "I think, however, that they would be better for relapse prevention as opposed to helping someone who smokes two packs a day. It would have to be someone who's already abstaining, and when that craving comes up and they have a cigarette—and then don't feel the effects of that cigarette—it would probably diminish their chance of relapse. The timing of when the vaccine dose is given will be very critical."

But there's a more immediate timing issue for Xenova: when it will enter the U.S. market and whether that will be soon enough to beat Nabi to the title of "first FDA-approved nicotine vaccine." As we saw with Viagra, being the first in a new class of pharmaceuticals is a huge advantage for the pioneering product, and, assuming there aren't any clinical-trial catastrophes, Nabi's NicVax is poised to be that product. NicVax is further along in its trials than Ta-Nic (phase 2 versus phase 1), thanks in part to the government funding. Xenova has received no such backing from Britain. As one drug-industry publication reported, "Full-scale trials are likely to prove too expensive for Xenova to fund solely, and it may seek a partner." Or hold one hell of a yard sale: This past August [2004], the company sold its manufacturing plant in Canada for $6 million.

The Federal Lawsuit Against Big Tobacco

Michael Janofsky and David Johnston

Following the historic tobacco settlement agreement in 1998 between forty-six states and the tobacco industry, the federal government under the Clinton administration launched a civil lawsuit against tobacco manufacturers to recoup millions lost in health care costs due to smoking. The U.S. Justice Department accused the industry of deceiving the public about the dangers of smoking and brought its case forward under a racketeering law originally intended to control organized crime. The government's lawsuit was dealt a blow early on when an appeals court ruled that the government could not seek back damages for smoking costs but only compensation to pay for smoking prevention and cessation programs. As a result, the amount of money the government could request from the industry was greatly reduced.

In the following article journalists Michael Janofsky and David Johnston analyze a startling decision made by the Justice Department in 2005 to reduce their claims against the tobacco industry from $130 billion to $10 billion. The writers imply that political pressure from the Bush administration may have played a role in the decision. As of June 2005 closing arguments in the case had been made and both sides were awaiting the U.S. district judge's decision. Michael Janofsky and David Johnston are Washington correspondents for the New York Times.

A Justice Department decision to seek $10 billion for a stop-smoking program in its suit against the country's leading tobacco companies, instead of the $130 billion suggested by one of its expert witnesses, set off a firestorm on Wednesday [June 8, 2005].

151

Several Democratic lawmakers with a longtime interest in smoking and health issues attacked the department for what they said was a politically motivated decision, as did public health groups.

Judge Gladys Kessler of Federal District Court, who is presiding in the trial here against the companies, took note of the sudden change, telling the court on Wednesday, "Perhaps it suggests that additional influences have been brought to bear on what the government's case is."

The move infuriated lawmakers who have long been critics of the tobacco industry. "It reeks of an administration whose heart isn't really in this case," said Senator Frank R. Lautenberg of New Jersey, at a news conference with other Democrats who suggested that Justice Department officials with ties to the tobacco industry might have grown uncomfortable with a large financial demand as part of the government's case against the companies.

The payments are intended to finance a stop-smoking program that a government witness said would cost $130 billion over 25 years. In court on Tuesday [June 7], a government lawyer, Stephen D. Brody, said the government would ask for a program costing only $10 billion to be paid out over five years.

In a statement issued Wednesday evening, the Justice Department said, "The government's suggested smoking cessation program is only an initial requirement, based on the compelling evidence that the defendants will continue to commit fraudulent acts in the future."

A department official said that $10 billion figure represented an effort to ask for an amount that would comply with adverse rulings by a court of appeals. "This is not politics," said the official. "This is exactly the contrary. This is trying to stay within the law and trying to stay within a decision with which we disagreed."

Despite the lower figure, if the judge, who is hearing the case without a jury, rules against the companies, she can impose financial penalties of any size, no matter what the government has requested.

The appeals decision cited by the administration official occurred five months into the trial. The ruling held that under civil racketeering laws, the tobacco companies could not be forced to relinquish past profits. Instead, the court said, the government could only seek sanctions that involved payments for new programs ordered by the judge.

Tobacco company lawyers expressed surprised delight at the change, saying they believed the government lawyers realized that Judge Kessler would not grant them as much as $130 billion.

The original figure was based on testimony from Dr. Michael C. Flore, an expert on tobacco addiction, who said an effective nationwide program that included a telephone helpline, access to medical treatment and counseling and a budget for advertising and promotion would cost $5.2 billion a year for 25 years.

"Why, in the middle of a lawsuit, would you give up, which is exactly what this administration has done?" said Senator Richard J. Durbin, Democrat of Illinois. "Was it because of the power of the tobacco lobby? Was it their close connection with people within the administration? Was it the fact that they'd never had the stomach to tackle this special interest group in Washington?" He added, "I think it's all of the above." . . .

William V. Corr, director of the Campaign for Tobacco-Free Kids, a health group that has fought the tobacco industry for years, said he and leaders of other antismoking groups, could only deduce from the retreat that the Bush administration did not want to inflict undue harm on the tobacco companies.

Taking on Tobacco

David Kessler was commmissioner of the Food and Drug Administration and instrumental in convincing President Clinton to bring federal charges in 1998 against the tobacco industry—leading to the federal racketeering trial still going on in 2005. In this excerpt, Kessler describes the power of the tobacco industry.

When we began our investigation of tobacco at the Food and Drug Administration, we had no idea of the power wielded by the tobacco companies, but we soon learned why the industry was for decades considered untouchable. Tobacco employed some of the most prestigious law firms in the country and commanded the allegiance of a significant section of the Congress. It also had access to the services of widely admired public figures, ranging from Prime Minister Margaret Thatcher to Senator Howard Baker. With its limitless resources and a corporate culture that was aggressively defensive, the industry perceived threats everywhere and responded to them ferociously.

David Kessler, A Question of Intent:
A Great American Battle with a Deadly
Industry. *New York: PublicAffairs, 2001.*

Here we are, at the last minute of the case, with senior political officials interfering with the trial team's materials and decisions," Mr. Corr said. Referring to antismoking groups, he added, "We've had a widespread sense since 2001 that the Bush administration was trying to kill the lawsuit."

The tobacco case, which was filed by President Bill Clinton's Justice Department in 1999, has been bathed in political intrigue since President Bush took office in 2001, setting off widespread speculation that the new administration had no real interest in pursuing a case against a big American industry.

Early in Mr. Bush's first term, his attorney general, John Ashcroft, revealed his discomfort with the lawsuit, moving to reduce financial support for the legal team in the case and pushing for a settlement because he viewed the case as weak.

Nonetheless, trial preparations continued for four years under a career prosecutor, Frank Marine, who guided a team of 35 department lawyers. By the start of the trial last September, the department said it had spent $135 million on the case.

Five months into the trial, the government suffered a major blow, when the United States Court of Appeals for the District of Columbia Circuit ruled that under civil racketeering laws, it was only entitled to seek sanctions, known as remedies, that were forward-looking, intended to prevent and restrain any future misconduct by the companies. As a result, the court said the $280 billion the government was seeking as profits from illegal activities was backward-looking and thus, unavailable.

On Wednesday, lawyers for all the tobacco companies took their turns in closing arguments, as, one by one, they tried to convince Judge Kessler that their clients did nothing over the years that could be construed as a racketeering violation.

David Bernick, a lawyer for Brown & Williamson, which merged last year [2004] with Reynolds, said at the outset, "The government's case is fatally flawed." He proceeded to argue that the government had failed to prove any of its claims against any of the defendant companies: Philip Morris; its parent, Altria; Brown & Williamson; Reynolds; Lorillard; Liggett; and Batco, a British company that no longer does business here.

Europe's First Smoking Ban

Patrick West

*Despite heavy opposition from bar owners and the tourist indus-
try, in 2004 Ireland banned smoking in all indoor places not
considered someone's home. In the following article written after
the announcement of the ban, Irish journalist Patrick West describes the mixed reaction of Irish citizens to the impending ban.
He expresses his surprise that the majority of the Irish seem to
be in favor of ending smoking in restaurants, bars, and other
public places. West also argues that Ireland is a "conformist nation" with a history of allowing the government to decide how
people should conduct their private lives. Nonetheless, West notes,
many people are likely to resent government intrusion into the
operations of the pub, a central institution in Irish life, and resist
the ban.*

*As of June 2005 Ireland's smoking ban has been declared an
undeniable success. Sales of cigarettes in pubs are down 60 percent, and the government reports a 97 percent compliance rate.
Although the sale of alcohol in pubs has fallen 6 percent, that
decline is partially attributed to the rising cost of alcohol. Neither the predicted widespread bar closures nor social rebellion
have taken place.*

In the imagination of many English people, the Irish are a
cheerful, rebellious folk who care little for officialdom, bad
government or oppressive laws. They are also deemed to pos-
sess the finest bars in the world, pubs that epitomise their he-
donistic, happy-go-lucky disposition.

This is the Ireland of [writer] Pete McCarthy's travelogues,
of television programmes such as *Ballykissangel* and *Father
Ted*, and countless newspaper travel pull-outs. Being half-Irish

Patrick West, "When Irish Eyes Are Spying," *New Statesman*, vol. 133, January 5,
2004, pp. 20–21. Copyright © 2005 by the New Statesman, Ltd. Reproduced by permission.

myself, I rather warm to these benign, if somewhat patronising, stereotypes. Alas, this rosy perception rings less true in reality today. Contemporary Ireland has, in one respect, one of the most illiberal governments in the western world, and a decidedly servile population to boot. And, travesty of travesties, Ireland may soon have the worst, most joyless pubs on the planet.

From 16 February [2004], it will be illegal to smoke in any restaurant or public house in the Republic of Ireland. No, this is not a joke. When you tell this to many English people, they assume that they have misheard you, or that you are pulling their leg. "Ireland? They're going to ban smoking in pubs in Ireland?" No, I didn't say Norway, Holland or New Zealand, places one would expect (and which shall shortly get) such interfering, state-sponsored hypochondria. No, I said Ireland.

Even if a ban were to be implemented, my English friends protest, surely the feisty, fun-loving Hibernians [the Latin name for Irish] would not pay attention to it? On the contrary, a majority of the Irish population appears to be in favour. A poll in the *Irish Independent* last year [2003] put the figure at almost 70 percent.

Among those who oppose the ban, there is a mood of acquiescence. Some smokers even feel a sneaking sense of gratitude towards the state.

"It'll be the end of the Irish pub," laments one punter [slang for gambler], pulling away on a fag [slang for cigarette] at the Rockland Hotel bar in Salthill, a suburb of Galway City. "It's all too far, too quick. People will simply stay at home instead." But not her. "I myself will be giving up. I couldn't stand the stress of having not to smoke in a bar." This sentiment is echoed by a barman in Jameson's, just up the road. "I'm a smoker myself, but I suppose I might as well give up when the smoking ban comes in. I don't like it, but I suppose it's going to happen."

The landlord [owner] of Killoran's Bar also says he may give up, but he has other worries. The new legislation places the burden not on the customer but on the landlord, so if a punter sparks up on his premises, the landlord is liable for a £1,900 fine [about $3,400] or a three-month jail sentence.

Many landlords fear unsavoury confrontations with their customers. "As if I'm going to tell a group of drunken young fellas to feckin' put out their fags," blusters the governor [manager] of Killoran's, "and get a punch in the face for my troubles."

The Impetus for the Ban

So why has the Irish state become so ferociously anti-smoking? It's partly down to the efforts of the health minister, Michael Martin. He once smoked a cigarette when he was 15, and so disgusted was he by the experience that he has since vowed to make Ireland "a tobacco-free country".

After commissioning a study from the grim-sounding Office of Tobacco Control which concluded that smoking was a hazard in the workplace, Martin announced that bar, hotel and restaurant staff should not have to be subjected to second-hand cigarette smoke. However, he magnanimously added that those who employ domestic cleaners will be permitted to smoke in their own homes.

This legislation makes California and New York City look positively anarchic. From next month [February 2004], only the mountain kingdom of Bhutan will have harsher anti-smoking laws (the king there has banned tobacco altogether). Martin proposes to set up a telephone hotline so that people can inform on the lawbreakers. It is hardly the stuff of tourist board brochures: "Come to Ireland! Don't enjoy 'the craic' [British slang for fun]! Spy on your neighbours!"

This is not just a case of the state working without the blessing of the populace. Compared with Britain, and for all its protestations about its leap into modernity, Ireland remains a conformist nation. Sure, councils [local governments] in London, Manchester, Sheffield and Brighton have made vague noises about implementing comparable bans in public places, but there would be outrage if the British government forced through a comparable law, bypassing parliament. After its tortured attempt to ban hunting with dogs, a pastime that has a vastly smaller number of people participating in it, the British government would surely be wary of taking on smokers.

Ireland may have unshackled itself from the Catholic Church, but it still has a puritan, finger-wagging elite that enjoys telling people how to conduct their private lives—and all this with the blessing of three-quarters of the populace, many of whom will tell you with a straight face that smoking should now be outlawed in homes and in private vehicles, "for our own good".

Those Who Will Resist the Ban

There is hope, however. Landlords in several counties in the old rebel strongholds of the west and south, including Galway, have announced that they will not observe the ruling. They say they will embark on a campaign of civil disobedience and are prepared to go to prison as a consequence. There are also reports from Donegal and Cavan that hotel functions planned for this year have been cancelled, with residents choosing instead to hold their parties across the border in Tyrone or Fermanagh. Thus, we now have the extraordinary situation of Catholics fleeing, in the belief that their rights are being infringed, into Northern Ireland.

Meanwhile, it has dawned on many erstwhile anti-smokers that the legislation is hopelessly ambitious. With crime, particularly violent crime, on the increase in the republic, it's not as if the police and the courts have not got enough to occupy themselves with. There is a growing realisation that this petty law is simply unworkable. Ireland is not the west coast of America: the pub is central to the Irish (and, indeed, British) way of life. As with fox-hunting, even some "antis" say that the government should really be devoting its energies to more pressing issues.

In the Bunch of Grapes in Galway City, the barman is convinced it is a non-starter. "It's not going to happen. Are you really going to have a situation where some old bloke who's been smoking for ages comes in and lights up, and someone is going to tell on him, or tell him to put it out?"

Let's hope he is right, for the sake of Ireland's bar staff, who might get cleaner air but would probably lose their jobs, and for the sake of the tourist industry, which is undoubtedly going to witness a downturn in fortunes.

But foremost, this legislation must be disobeyed to save the reputation of the Irish, who have always been admired as a people that love a good time and hate stupid laws. What a tragedy it would be if the country that gave us James Joyce, Brendan Behan and Shane MacGowan [Irish writers and musicians] should end up as a joyless Bhutan-on-Sea.

Banning Smoking in the United States

Mark Sappenfield

In this article writer Mark Sappenfield describes the growing drive to ban smoking in workplaces and public spaces. Smoking is already prohibited in restaurants, bars, and workplaces in ten states, and twenty more states may consider such bans in 2005. Sappenfield also reports that many large corporations have begun charging higher health premiums for smokers and that some companies are even refusing to hire those who smoke. These companies' policies are legal in the states in which they have gone into effect because the courts have ruled that the Constitution does not protect smokers and that each state legislature has the right to determine what protections smokers will be granted. Mark Sappenfield is a staff writer for the Christian Science Monitor.

Fifteen years after antismoking forces struck their first major blow [in 1990], the drive to make workplaces and public spaces across the United States smoke-free is experiencing a new surge.

In February 1990, airlines for the first time outlawed smoking on flights lasting less than six hours. This year [2005], legislators have proposed far-reaching public smoking bans in nine states, with similar legislation expected in as many as 11 more. In other states, large cities such as Houston and Salt Lake are considering bans of their own—including one here [in San Francisco] that would prohibit smoking even in parks.

The push comes at a time when businesses are already targeting smokers in an effort to bring down healthcare costs. Some corporations are refusing to hire smokers—or firing them. A larger number are putting increasing emphasis on counseling and stop-smoking programs, even as they ban smoking anywhere on their property.

In many ways, all the activity is simply the continuation of a long-term trend, as cities and companies gradually impose more smoking restrictions. But as these bans push further into everyday life, this year's increased activity suggests that the issue might be nearing a hinge-point when Americans will define the limits of how far antismoking policies can go.

"This is the direction things are headed in," says Paula Brantner of Workplace Fairness, an advocate for worker's rights. "It may not stop in progressive states until the only place you can smoke is your home."

For some companies, even that is not enough. Late last month [January 2005], a Michigan company made national news by firing four workers who refused to submit to a nicotine test. Alaska Airlines has a policy of not hiring smokers. Union Pacific railroad recently began a policy of rejecting all work applications by smokers.

It's Not Personal

In a time when companies are straining to meet rising healthcare costs, the rationale is purely financial. "The basic idea is that smokers have higher healthcare costs than nonsmokers," says John Bromley, a spokesman for Union Pacific in Omaha, Neb. According to company estimates, he adds, each smoking employee costs $922 more per year than a nonsmoking employee.

In 21 states, the policy is perfectly legal. Courts have decided that the Constitution does not protect smokers, leaving it up to each state legislature to determine protections. In the early 1990s, 29 states passed laws protecting smokers from discrimination, and Union Pacific's policy, for example, only applies to workers not in those states.

Yet even in those other 21 states, Union Pacific's stand tips toward the extreme. While there is little data on American firms' policies toward smokers, one recent poll suggests that only 1 percent of businesses refuse to hire smokers and only 5 percent prefer to not hire smokers. After all, smokers still make up 23 percent of the adult population—though that is down from 37 percent in 1970.

"[Companies] want to encourage healthy behavior instead of punishing," says Rebecca Hastings of the Society for Human Resource Management in Alexandria, Va., which conducted the poll.

According to the survey, 5 percent of companies have taken the slightly softer approach of passing on higher healthcare premiums to employees who smoke. Smokers who work at U-Haul International, for instance, must pay $11.50 a week to participate in a wellness program. But that can be a slippery slope.

"Then they should also charge for employees who engage in other forms of risky behavior," says Lew Maltby of the Workrights Institute in Princeton, N.J. "Everything you do in your private life affects your health."

The greater movement is to encourage all employees to live healthier lifestyles, with particular attention paid to smokers.

"There's a lot more effort to help people quit smoking," says Helen Darling of the National Business Group on Health in Washington. "And more companies will not allow smoking anywhere on the campus—that's a trend."

It is also a vanguard of the antismoking laws now advancing through state legislatures nationwide. In the 11 years since California first instituted a ban on smoking in restaurants and bars, a handful of states have considered similar restrictions each year. So far, measures to prohibit smoking in restaurants, bars, or workplaces have taken effect in 10 states.

As many as 20 states may take up the issue this year [2005]. "This hasn't really happened before," says Bronson Frick of the American Nonsmokers' Rights Foundation in Berkeley, Calif.

He expects most bills to fail, but the fact that antismoking laws are being considered in states such as Georgia and North Carolina represents progress to him. Add to that the cities that have already passed workplace bans—including Laramie, Wyo., and Lincoln, Neb.—and he sees an expanding antismoking imprint. "The political will is changing," says Mr. Frick.

On the West Coast

Leading the way, not surprisingly, is San Francisco. Last year [2004], several coastal cities in southern California went so far as to ban smoking on public beaches. This year, San Francisco supervisors passed a law—supported by the mayor—that will prohibit smoking in all city-run recreational areas except golf courses.

That includes Mission Dolores Park—and Daniel Lopez. On a cloudless morning, Mr. Lopez and a friend sit on a bench atop the park's grassy ridge, looking out over the skyline of San Francisco—the city framed by a stand of palm trees and smudged by the white thumbprint of a stubborn postdawn haze.

The turquoise lighter in Lopez's hand betrays that he is a smoker, but when he learns of the new smoking ban—which should go into effect July 1—he defends it, while his friend rails against it.

"The next thing they'll tell me is that I can't wear shorts," says his friend, Marty Soni.

Speaking with the earnest tone of one bestowing great wisdom, Lopez answers: "It's not too much to ask for preservation. I'd probably forget, but I'd do my best to try to abide by it."

Farther down the hill, au pair Simona Piazza tends to her tiny charge, an infant nestled in a stroller taking mouthfuls of baby food. She, too, is a smoker. And she, too, supports the law. "Other people should have a chance to breathe fresh air," she says.

To be sure, San Francisco is a different sort of place, where self-awareness seems to be written into the city charter. But Lopez and Ms. Piazza also suggest how far the public debate has shifted in recent years.

"When this all started, people thought it was unacceptable to ban smoking at work," says Ms. Brantner of Workplace Fairness. These days, "it's not popular to defend smoking."

Appendix A

How Drugs Are Classified

The Controlled Substances Act of 1970 classified drugs into five different lists, or schedules, in order of decreasing potential for abuse. The decision to place a drug on a particular schedule is based mainly on the effects the drug has on the body, mind, and behavior. However, other factors are also considered. The schedule is used to help establish the penalties for someone using or selling illegal drugs. On the other hand, sometimes a potentially valuable drug for treating a disease can be incorrectly scheduled, greatly hampering the exploration of its usefulness as a treatment.

Schedule of Controlled Substances

Rating	Example
Schedule I A high potential for abuse; no currently accepted medical use in the United States; or no accepted safety for use in treatment under medical supervision.	• Heroin • LSD • Marijuana • Mescaline • MDMA (Ectasy) • PCP
Schedule II A high potential for abuse; currently accepted medical use with severe restrictions; abuse of the substance may lead to severe psychological or physical dependence.	• Opium and Opiates • Codeine • Percodan • Methamphetamines • Cocaine • Amphetamines
Schedule III A potential for abuse less than the substances listed in Schedules I and II; currently accepted medical use in the United States; abuse may lead to moderate or low physical dependence or high psychological dependence.	• Anabolic steriods • Hydrocodone • Certain barbiturates • Hallucinogenic substances
Schedule IV A low potential for abuse relative to the substances listed in Schedule III; currently accepted medical use in the United States; limited physical or psychological dependence relative to the substances listed in Schedule III.	• Barbiturates • Narcotics • Stimulants
Schedule V A low potential for abuse relative to the substances listed in Schedule III; currently accepted medical use in the United States; limited physical or psychological dependence relative to the substances listed in Schedule IV.	• Compounds with limited codeine such as cough medicine.

Appendix B

Facts About Nicotine

Nicotine is the active ingredient contained in the tobacco plant.

Most tobacco products available in the twenty-first century are of the tobacco variety of *Nicotiana tabacum.*

Nicotine can be ingested by smoking dried tobacco, chewing dried tobacco, or allowing tobacco to sit in the mouth so that the nicotine is absorbed through the mucous membranes.

Many researchers agree that both nicotine and the physical act of smoking are addictive.

Inhaled nicotine takes about ten seconds to reach the brain, providing a brief feeling of elation, also called a high or rush, as the pleasure centers in the brain are stimulated.

The effects of a cigarette wear off about one hour after the last inhale.

The larger, thicker cigar differs from the cigarette in that many cigar smokers merely draw the smoke into their mouths and release it, rather than inhaling it into the lungs, as is the practice in cigarette smoking.

Many cigarette users report both a stimulant and a depressant effect. A person may smoke in the morning to help wake up, and also in the evening to relax.

Most researchers agree that extensive use of nicotine and tobacco causes myriad diseases including cancer, heart disease, lung disease, low fetal birth weight, and stroke.

Tobacco was used by Native Americans since its first suspected cultivation around 400 B.C. for spiritual and medicinal purposes.

Throughout history, tobacco has been used as currency.

Nicotine is one of the most heavily used drugs in the United States.

Since the beginning of the twentieth century, cigarette smoking remains the most popular method of ingesting nicotine. In the twenty-first century, 96 percent of tobacco users smoke cigarettes.

By the end of World War II, 75 percent of the male population of the United States smoked on a regular basis.

Of adult smokers, 80 percent began smoking under the age of eighteen.

Tobacco is the most widely grown nonfood crop in the world.

China is the largest grower of tobacco in the world.

Most of the tobacco produced in the United States is grown in North and South Carolina, Virginia, and Maryland.

To prepare tobacco for smoking, it must be "cured," or dried after harvest, then shredded.

Most experts agree that tobacco-related health problems cost the United States $75 billion per year in direct medical costs.

Tobacco companies manufacture 5.5 trillion cigarettes a year worldwide.

Philip Morris is the world's largest international tobacco manufacturer.

Brazil is the largest exporter of tobacco leaf in the world; Russia and the United States are the largest importers.

Chronology

1492

The crew of Spanish explorer Christopher Columbus discovers tobacco in use by Native Americans in the New World. Columbus brings tobacco back with him to Europe, where it quickly becomes popular.

1604

King James I of England writes *A Counterblaste to Tobacco*, one of the first antismoking documents.

1607

The first substantial cultivation of tobacco by Europeans in the New World is begun in Jamestown. Tobacco quickly becomes the major cash crop of the colonies for export to England.

1665

The Great Plague envelops Europe. Smoking, thought to ward off the disease, is made compulsory at Eton.

1730

The first American tobacco factory, making snuff, is opened in Virginia.

1794

The U.S. Congress passes the first excise tax on tobacco products.

1828

Hand-rolled cigarettes become popular in Europe.

1843

The French company SEITA begins the large scale manufacture of cigarettes.

1858

Fears about the health risks of smoking are first raised in the *Lancet,* a British medical journal.

1862

The U.S. government places the first federal tax on the sale of raw tobacco, raising $3 million to help pay for the Civil War.

1913

American tobacco manufacturer R.J. Reynolds introduces "Camels," the first prepackaged, preblended cigarette, ushering in the age of modern cigarette smoking.

1918

Cigarettes are included in rations for American soldiers fighting in World War I.

1929

Public smoking for women becomes acceptable with the launch of a major advertising and public relations campaign by ad man Edward Bernays.

1933

The U.S. Congress passes the Agricultural Adjustment Act, which provides price supports for tobacco farmers struggling during the Great Depression.

1945

During World War II, President Roosevelt makes tobacco a protected crop. So many cigarettes are sent to troops overseas that there is a national shortage.

1950

The first clinical study linking smoking to lung cancer is published in the *Journal of the American Medical Association* by physician Morton Levin.

1952

Filtered cigarettes are developed by the tobacco company Lorillard when it introduces the "Micronite" filter on its Kent brand cigarettes.

The health risks of smoking are introduced to the general public when *Reader's Digest* publishes "Cancer by the Carton" by Roy Norr.

1954

The Tobacco Industry Research Committee (TIRC) is founded by tobacco companies to counteract increasing claims of health risks associated with smoking.

1964

Surgeon General Luther Terry issues his landmark report "Smoking and Health," which begins the modern antismoking movement in the United States. Tobacco sales begin a decline from which they have never recovered.

1965

The first "Surgeon General's Warnings" appear on cigarette packs, as ordered by Congress.

1971

The U.S. government bans cigarette advertising on television and radio.

1977

The American Cancer Society holds the first Great American Smokeout, during which all citizens are encouraged to stop smoking for twenty-four hours.

1984

The Food and Drug Administration (FDA) approves Nicorette, a nicotine gum created to aid smoking cessation.

1989

Smoking is banned on all U.S. domestic airlines.

1992

The transdermal nicotine patch, Nicoderm, is introduced to the public to aid smoking cessation.

1994

Mississippi is the first state to sue tobacco companies to regain some of the health-care costs associated with smoking. Eventually forty-six states will sue tobacco companies to recoup these health-care costs.

1995

The FDA classifies nicotine as a drug.

1998

Forty-six states settle with tobacco companies in the Master Settlement agreement. Two hundred and six billion dollars will be paid by the tobacco industry to the states over twenty-five years.

1999

The federal government under the Clinton administration files a $22 billion civil lawsuit against major tobacco companies to recoup health-care costs associated with smoking. The Philip Morris tobacco company acknowledges the link between smoking and cancer.

2003

Ireland becomes the first European country to implement a nationwide public smoking ban. In the United States, Dallas, Boston, and New York City follow suit.

2005

Closing arguments are heard in the federal tobacco lawsuit; the U.S. District Court has not yet made its decision.

Organizations to Contact

Action on Smoking and Health (ASH)
2013 H St. NW, Washington, DC 20006
(202) 659-4310
Web site: www.ash.org

Action on Smoking and Health is a nonprofit organization created to protect the rights of nonsmokers. The organization's primary goal is to end all government support of the tobacco industry and serve as a clearinghouse for antitobacco information. ASH maintains an antismoking information Web site and publishes a bimonthly magazine, *Smoking and Health Review;* a report on the effects of secondhand smoke; and forms to guide members who wish to appeal to their senators and congressional representatives to pass antismoking legislation.

American Cancer Society (ACS)
1599 Clifton Rd. NE, Atlanta, GA 30329
(800) 227-2345
Web site: www.cancer.org

The American Cancer Society is a national nonprofit organization that provides information, advice, and services to those afflicted by and concerned about cancer. ACS, the creator of the Great American Smokeout—a national day of smoking awareness—believes that smoking is one of the primary preventable causes of cancer and seeks to educate the public about the dangers of tobacco use. The organization publishes numerous pamphlets, videos, and books, including *Kicking Butts: Quit Smoking and Take Charge of Your Health.*

American Legacy Foundation (ALF)
2030 M St. NW, 6th Fl., Washington, DC 20036
(202) 454-5555 • fax: (202) 454-5599
e-mail: info@americanlegacy.org

Web site: www.americanlegacy.org

Founded in the wake of the tobacco settlement of the 1990s, in which tobacco companies paid billions of dollars to compensate states for the health care costs of smoking, and funded primarily by the settlement payments, this national, independent public health foundation's goal is to educate America's youth about the dangers of tobacco and to encourage equal access for all to tobacco cessation services. ALF focuses on public awareness campaigns and grassroots efforts to reach groups in which tobacco use is highest. In addition to policy reports on tobacco issues, including *Saving Lives, Saving Money: Why States Should Invest in a Tobacco-Free Future,* the foundation also publishes *First Look* reports that summarize the foundation's most recent efforts and information.

American Lung Association (ALA)

61 Broadway, 6th Fl.
   New York, NY 10006
(800) 586-4872
Web site: www.lungusa.org

The American Lung Association is a national nonprofit health organization that works to increase public awareness about a variety of issues related to lung disease. Tobacco regulation is a major component of the association's public awareness programs. On its Web site ALA provides resources to fight smoking on different levels, including a smoking cessation program and legal and governmental information about the tobacco lobby. ALA publishes an online newsletter, *The Weekly Breather.*

Americans for Nonsmokers' Rights (ANR)

2530 San Pablo Ave., Suite J
   Berkeley, CA 94702
(510) 841-3032 • fax: (510) 841-3071
Web site: www.no-smoke.org

ANR is a national lobbying organization that works to defend the rights of nonsmokers at all levels of government, focusing its efforts mainly on combating the tobacco industry. The group provides a forum for nonsmokers to discuss issues of importance, lobbies Congress to pass antismoking legislation, and supports litigation against the tobacco industry. ANR publishes *Update,* an e-mail newsletter.

Campaign for Tobacco-Free Kids

1400 Eye St. NW, Suite 1200
  Washington, DC 20005
(202) 296-5496 • fax: (202) 296-5427
e-mail: info@tobaccofreekids.org
Web site: www.tobaccofreekids.org

The Campaign for Tobacco-Free Kids is a nongovernmental initiative founded to discourage young people from smoking and to track and report on tobacco industry efforts to target children and teenagers in advertising. The campaign works to influence government at the local, state, and national level to create policies to protect children from tobacco. The initiative publishes "special reports" on current tobacco issues, including *Big Tobacco: Still Addicting Kids,* and *Tobacco-Free E-News,* its online newsletter.

FORCES International

PO Box 14347, San Francisco, CA 94114
(415) 675-0157
e-mail: info@forces.org
Web site: www.forces.org

FORCES (Fight Ordinances and Restrictions to Control and Eliminate Smoking) is a nonprofit advocacy group that works for consumers' rights, including smokers. The organization attempts to prevent and repeal all smoking bans, to correct what it sees as misunderstandings about the dangers of secondhand smoke, and to end all government restrictions on tobacco and government support of antitobacco groups. FORCES maintains an online archive and news database of materials relevant to its mission.

International Tobacco Growers' Association (ITGA)
30 Avenue General Humberto Delgado
   Castelo Branco 6000-081
   Portugal
(351) 272-325-901 • fax: (351) 272-325-209
e-mail: itga@tobaccoleaf.org
Web site: www.tobaccoleaf.org

ITGA is a nonprofit organization founded in 1984 and based in Portugal. The association works to present the cause of tobacco growers worldwide. The group attempts to counteract international antitobacco growing campaigns and provides a forum in which growers can share advice and information and monitor market conditions. The ITGA publishes a quarterly newsletter, *The Tobacco Courier,* as well as various reports and issue papers, including *Tobacco Farming: Sustainable Alternatives?* and *Tobacco in the Developing World.*

National African American Tobacco Education Network (NAATEN)
3950 Industrial Blvd., Suite 600
   West Sacramento, CA 95691
(916) 556-3344 • fax: 916-446-0427
e-mail: naaten@healthedcouncil.org
Web site: www.naaten.org

NAATEN is a network of several national groups concerned with the health of African Americans and the influence of tobacco on the African American community. Its mission is to reduce the instances of tobacco use by African Americans by providing a national voice for antitobacco groups and by uniting African American organizations to prevent smoking. The organization publishes an e-mail newsletter, *Just-US Against Tobacco.*

Nicotine Anonymous (NA)
419 Main St., PMB# 370
   Huntington Beach, CA 92648
(415) 750-0328
e-mail: info@nicotine-anonymous.org

Web site: www.nicotine-anonymous.org

Nicotine Anonymous is a twelve-step program for smokers who wish to quit. The group is structured like Alcoholics Anonymous. Addicts meet in groups where they share their experiences in an anonymous environment. NA publishes a variety of pamphlets outlining the twelve-step program, including *Tips for Gaining Freedom from Nicotine.*

Tobacco Associates (TA)
1725 K St. NW, Suite 512
  Washington, DC 20006
(202) 828-9144 • fax: (202) 828-9149
e-mail: taw@tobaccoassociatesinc.org
Web site: www.tobaccoassociatesinc.org

Tobacco Associates, a nonprofit organization funded by tobacco farmers, was created to encourage U.S. tobacco manufacturers to use domestic tobacco in their products. The group's mission is to promote the use of flue-cured tobacco and to provide information for tobacco manufacturers interested in using domestic tobacco. TA holds seminars and outreach programs and publishes a range of multimedia materials intended to market U.S. tobacco.

For Further Research

Books

Walter Adams, *The Tobacco Wars.* Cincinnati, OH: South Western Press, 1999.

Allan Brandt, *Rise and Fall of the Cigarette: A Cultural History of Smoking in the U.S.* New York: Basic Books, 1999.

Harold Cordry, *Tobacco: A Reference Handbook.* Santa Barbara, CA: ABC-CLIO, 2001.

Martha Derthick, *Up in Smoke: From Legislation to Litigation in Tobacco Politics.* Washington, DC: CQ Press, 2005.

Craig Donnellan, *The Smoking Debate.* Cambridge, UK: Independence, 2002.

John Fahs, *Cigarette Confidential: The Unfiltered Truth About the Ultimate American Addiction.* Berkeley, CA: Berkeley, 1996.

Iain Gately, *Tobacco: The Story of How Tobacco Seduced the World.* New York: Grove Press, 2001.

Sander Gilman, *Smoke: A Global History of Smoking.* London: Reaktion, 2004.

Stanton Glantz, *The Cigarette Papers.* Berkeley: University of California Press, 1996.

Simon Gray, *The Smoking Diaries.* London: Granta Books, 2004.

Philip Hilts, *Smokescreen: The Truth Behind the Tobacco Industry Cover Up.* Reading, MA: Addison Wesley, 1996.

David Kessler, *A Question of Intent: A Great American Battle with a Deadly Industry.* New York: PublicAffairs, 2001.

Judith Mackay, *The Tobacco Atlas.* Geneva, Switzerland: World Health Organization, 2002.

Fred Pampel, *The Tobacco Industry and Smoking.* New York: Facts On File, 2004.

Tara Parker-Pope, *Cigarettes: An Anatomy of an Industry from Seed to Smoke.* New York: New Press, 2001.

Chris Proctor, *Sometimes a Cigarette Is Just a Cigarette.* London: Sinclair-Stevenson, 2003.

Robert Rabin, *Regulating Tobacco.* Oxford, UK: Oxford University Press, 2001.

Frank Sloan, *The Price of Smoking.* Cambridge, MA: MIT Press, 2004.

Paul Slovic, *Smoking: Risk, Perception & Policy.* Thousand Oaks, CA: Sage, 2001.

Argus Thompson, *The Tobacco Industry: Wheezing or Breathing?* Hauppauge, NY: Nova Science, 2002.

W. Kip Viscusi, *Smoke-Filled Rooms: A Postmortem on the Tobacco Deal.* Chicago: University of Chicago Press, 2002.

Mark Wolfson, *The Fight Against Big Tobacco: The Movement, the State, and the Public's Health.* New York: Aldine de Gruyter, 2001.

Dan Zegart, *Civil Warriors: The Legal Siege on the Tobacco Industry.* New York: Delacorte Press, 2000.

Periodicals

Benoit Aubin, "Saying No to Cigarettes," *Maclean's,* January 24, 2005.

Christopher Bailey Jr., "From 'Informed Choice,' to 'Social Hygiene': Government Control of Cigarette Smoking in the U.S.," *Journal of American Studies,* April 2004.

Beryl Bainbridge, "Life, Death, and Cigarettes," *New States-man,* May 3, 2004.

Bob Barr, "Tobacco 'Settlement' Sends Much More than Cigarettes Up in Smoke," *Human Events,* July 25, 1997.

Lisa Bero, "Tobacco Industry Manipulation of Research," *Public Health Reports,* March/April 2005.

Joanna Blythman, "The New Tobacco," *Ecologist,* November 2004.

Sean Bruich, "Target for Nicotine Addiction Found," *Science Now,* November 5, 2004.

Monte Burke, "Blowing Smoke," *Forbes,* December 11, 2000.

Andy Coghlan, "Nicotine Speeds the Growth of Lung Cancers," *New Scientist,* March 29, 2003.

————, "No Limit to Tobacco's Harm," *New Scientist,* June 5, 2004.

Ann Cook, "Smoking Cessation: What Really Works?" *Pulse,* March 29, 2004.

Mary Cooper, "Tobacco Industry," *CQ Researcher,* December 10, 2004.

Robert Davis and Debra Goldschmidt, "Weighing Issues on Smokeless Tobacco," *Wall Street Journal,* April 26, 2005.

Roddy Doyle, "Cigarettes Are Sexy," *British Medical Journal,* August 1999.

Amy Fairchild, "Out of the Ashes: The Life, Death, and Rebirth of the 'Safer' Cigarette in the United States," *American Journal of Public Health,* February 2004.

Dean Foust and Nanette Byrnes, "The High Cost of Nicotine Withdrawal," *Business Week,* May 23, 2005.

Liesa Goins, "The Cost of Smoking," *Men's Health,* November 2004.

Lila Guterman, "The Medicinal Value of Nicotine (Really)," *Chronicle of Higher Education,* March 17, 2000.

Susan Hayes, "Nicotine Patch and Women," *Prevention,* January 2005.

Katherine Hobson, "Quit Smoking," *U.S. News & World Report,* December 27, 2004.

Marianne Hurst, "Smoking and Academics," *Education Week,* June 23, 2004.

Sarah Jarvis, "Tobacco or Health? Physiological and Social Damages Caused by Tobacco Smoking," *Update,* January 20, 2005.

Sharon Kingman, "Smoking Shortens Life by Decade, Concludes 50-Year Study," *Bulletin of the World Health Organization,* August 2004.

Michele Late, "Millions Could Quit Smoking If Given the Right Help," *Nation's Health,* March 2004.

Shawn Macomber, "Relighting the Tobacco Wars," *American Spectator,* July/August 2004.

N. Gerry McElvaney, "Smoking Ban—Made in Ireland, for Home Use and for Export," *New England Journal of Medicine,* May 27, 2004.

Neil Munro, "No Juice for Smokeless Tobacco," *National Journal,* June 14, 2003.

Vanessa O'Connell, "Marlboro Cigarette Avoids 'Safer' Claim, but Scrutiny Arises," *Wall Street Journal,* January 21, 2005.

Diana Parsell, "Nicotine's Good Side," *Science News,* November 6, 2004.

Dennis Ranalli, "Spit Tobacco," *Scholastic Coach & Athletic Director,* April 1996.

David Satcher, "Cigars and Public Health," *New England Journal of Medicine,* June 10, 1999.

Richard Schickel, "Caffeine and Nicotine," *Science Now,* May 24, 2004.

Stacey Schultz, "Would-Be Quitters Get Help Winning Against Nicotine," *U.S. News & World Report,* May 29, 2000.

Sora Song, "Smoking Hits Women Harder," *Time,* December 8, 2003.

Karen Springen, "Women, Cigarettes, and Death," *Newsweek,* May 10, 2004.

Jacob Sullum, "Cowboys, Camels, and Kids," *Reason,* April 1998.

———, "Nicotine Fights," *Reason,* May 2003.

Namrita Talwar, "Taking the World up in Smoke: A Tobacco Peril," *UN Chronicle,* June–August, 2004.

Stuart Taylor Jr., "The Vast Tobacco Anti-Trust Conspiracy— and How to Break It," *National Journal,* October 7, 2000.

Michael Tennesen and Sad Harrar, "Nicotine Low, Danger High," *Prevention,* September 2002.

Ray Thorpe, "Addictive Cigarettes," *New Internationalist,* October 2004.

Michael Thun, "When Truth Is Unwelcome: The First Reports on Smoking and Lung Cancer," *Bulletin of the World Health Organization,* February 2005.

Clare Wilson, "My Friend Nicotine," *New Scientist,* November 10, 2001.

Derek Yach, "Tobacco: Science, Policy, and Public Health," *Bulletin of the World Health Organization,* May 2005.

Cecil Yancey, "The Tobacco Buyout," *Southeast Farm Press,* December 15, 2004.

Index